CONTEMPORARY CASE STUDIES

# Food & Famine

## Michael Witherick

Series editor: Sue Warn

Philip Allan Updates, an imprint of Hodder Education, an Hachette UK company, Market Place, Deddington, Oxfordshire OX15 0SE

*Orders*

Bookpoint Ltd, 130 Milton Park, Abingdon, Oxfordshire, OX14 4SB
tel: 01235 827720
fax: 01235 400454
e-mail: uk.orders@bookpoint.co.uk

Lines are open 9.00 a.m.–5.00 p.m., Monday to Saturday, with a 24-hour message answering service. You can also order through the Philip Allan Updates website: www.philipallan.co.uk

© Philip Allan Updates 2010

ISBN 978-0-340-99182-4

First printed 2010
Impression number 5 4 3 2 1
Year 2015 2014 2013 2012 2011 2010

Front cover photograph Friedrich Stark/Alamy

Printed in Italy

Hachette UK's policy is to use papers that are natural, renewable and recyclable products and made from wood grown in sustainable forests. The logging and manufacturing processes are expected to conform to the environmental regulations of the country of origin.

P01662

# Contents

# Part 3: Famine and life on the margins

# Part 4: Power players in the global food chain

# Part 5: The environmental impacts of food production

# Introduction

Food is the staff of life. It is arguably the greatest human need. This book focuses on the **human food chain** that exists to meet this most basic of needs. The chain involves four critical processes, namely the production, processing, distribution and consumption of food. We are constantly reminded that we live in an unequal world. Perhaps the cruellest global inequality of all is that produced by the mismatch between two critical processes, namely the demand for food (i.e. consumption) and the supply of food (production). As a consequence, there are parts of the world where the supply is so inadequate that human health is threatened. Equally, there are parts where the supply is so abundant that human health is also at risk, but in a rather different way. So the global inequality in focus throughout this book can be described by a number of contrasting terms — **malnutrition** and **overnutrition**, **famine** and **feast**, **food insecurity** and **food security**. These pairings clearly indicate that all is not well with one of the processes making the critical link between **food production** and food consumption — distribution.

## About this book

This book focuses on seven different aspects of the production and consumption of food:

**Part 1** is concerned with the global patterns of food production and consumption, and how both processes have changed over time.

**Part 2** looks at the mismatch between food production and consumption and the resulting global patterns of food security and insecurity.

**Part 3** investigates the causes of famine and the nature of life at the margins of survival.

**Figure 1**
*The food production and consumption chain*

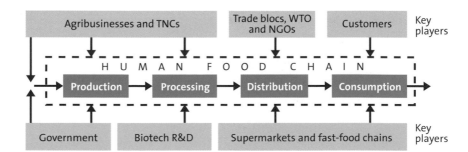

**Part 4** puts the spotlight on modern food production and its key players, namely transnational companies, agribusiness and politicians.

**Part 5** examines the diverse environmental impacts of modern food production.

**Part 6** looks at strategies to raise food production and food security in the developing world. Is it possible to achieve these objectives in a **sustainable** way?

**Part 7** discusses some broader issues relating to food security that have a global significance.

Each of these parts provides the context for a selection of related case studies. At the end of many of them, the key points are summarised in italics. Some of the case studies are followed by 'Using case studies' boxes. These set a range of related questions and tasks. Guidance is given on how they might be tackled. They all aim to improve your comprehension and use of case studies so that you can enrich and support your examination answers and coursework with real-world examples.

The final part of the book (**Part 8**) consolidates much of this advice and gives some additional tips on making the most of your case study material in the examination.

# Key terms

**Agribusiness:** a large-scale farming system run on business lines, with interests in both 'upstream' inputs (seeds, fertilisers, feedstuffs and machinery) and 'downstream' outputs (food processing and marketing).

**Agrochemicals:** a term used to cover all chemicals used in modern agriculture, namely fertilisers, fungicides, herbicides and insecticides.

**Aquaculture:** the management of water environments (marine and freshwater) with a view to producing and harvesting animals (fish and crustaceans) and plants (seaweeds). Commonly referred to as 'fish farming'.

**Carrying capacity:** the maximum number of people that can be supported by a given resource or in a given area in a sustainable way that does not prejudice or degrade the environment.

**Collective farming:** a type of agricultural organisation introduced in Russia after the Bolshevik Revolution and subsequently in other communist countries. While the land is state-owned, it is leased to a large group of workers who run it as a single farm-holding and are obliged to sell its produce at a low price set by the state. Any profits from such sales are shared equally by collective members.

**Commercial farming:** agricultural practices and systems producing commodities (crops, livestock by-products) that are sold for profit.

**Daily calorie intake per person:** the number of calories that need to be consumed each day in order to sustain the body in good health. The number varies from person to person and with latitude.

**Desertification:** the process by which land becomes drier and degraded, as a result of climate change or human factors, or both.

**Diet:** the average food intake of people and its typical components (nutrients).

**Drip irrigation:** an irrigation method which drip-feeds water directly to the roots of plants through a network of valves and pipes. Also known as trickle irrigation, it saves water (by curbing evaporation) and fertilisers (by preventing them from being washed out).

**Drylands:** ecosystems characterised by a lack of water. They include cultivated lands, scrublands, grasslands, savannas, semi-deserts and true deserts.

**Eutrophication:** the process whereby nutrient enrichment leads to the reduction of oxygen in streams, rivers and lakes and the consequent death of fish, molluscs and other species.

**Famine:** a chronic shortage of food in which many people die from starvation.

**Feast:** circumstances in which people can indulge in excessive eating.

**Food availability deficit:** a situation in which there is not enough food to feed all those who need it.

**Food consumption:** the intake of food (both natural and processed) and liquids necessary to sustain human life.

**Food entitlement deficit:** a situation in which sufficient food may be available, but people are unable to access it for reasons of cost and poverty.

**Food insecurity:** a situation in which the people of a given area do not have access to an adequate supply of food, or the supply of food fluctuates on a seasonal or annual basis.

**Food miles:** how far food travels from the farmer who produces it to the consumer who eats it.

**Food production:** a term to describe food derived from all sources, from arable and livestock farming to fishing and **aquaculture**.

**Food security:** the availability of food in a given area and the ability of all individuals to access food supplies.

**Gene Revolution:** a term used to describe current developments in biotechnology which involve the genetic modification of crops and livestock in order to increase **food production** and **food security**.

**Genome:** the genetic material that carries the inherited characteristics of an organism.

**GM crops/food:** the product of genetic engineering undertaken to increase the productivity, quality, and disease or drought resistance of crops and livestock.

**Globesity:** the sudden and widespread surge in personal weight levels resulting from overnutrition and lack of exercise. Now regarded as a pandemic.

**Green Revolution:** a term used to describe new farming technology introduced in the early 1960s. It involved new high-yielding strains of cereals (rice and wheat), as well as fertilisers, irrigation and mechanisation. It was hoped that these developments would raise **food production** in developing countries.

**Human food chain:** the succession of processes that links **food production** and **food consumption**.

**Hunger:** a need for, or lack, of food.

**Industrialisation:** in the context of **food production**, this means mechanisation and a business approach that reaps the benefits of scale economies.

**Intermediate technology:** low-technology solutions that are often cheap, labour-intensive and easy to build and maintain, as well as adaptable to local conditions. It is generally considered to be environmentally friendly.

**Land grabbing:** a process whereby richer countries acquire land in poor countries, mainly for producing food but also for growing biofuel crops.

**Malnutrition:** an imbalance between what a person eats and what is needed to maintain good health; the outcome of a **diet** persistently lacking critical nutrients.

**Obesity:** a medical condition in which excess body fat has accumulated to the extent that it may have an adverse effect on health, leading to reduced life expectancy.

**Outsourcing:** a process whereby rich countries look to poorer ones to produce their food and provide other commodities.

**Overnutrition:** the condition in which food nutrients are oversupplied in relation to the amounts required for normal growth, development and metabolism. It is regarded by some as a form of **malnutrition**.

**Overpopulation:** a condition in which the population of an area exceeds the **carrying capacity** of that area. The population therefore cannot be adequately supported by the available resources, technology and methods of production.

**Permaculture:** a type of intensive agriculture that is both high-yielding and sustainable because it is based on, and takes advantage of, natural ecological processes.

**Restructuring:** making basic alterations to the economic activities and even the whole economy of a country. It is undertaken principally to increase productivity and to take advantage of new opportunities.

**Salinisation:** a form of land degradation that occurs in arid and semi-arid areas. It involves the accumulation of salts in the soil, as when evaporation and transpiration are greater than precipitation. It is increasingly associated with irrigation and with over-pumping of groundwater, which draws in sea water.

**Starvation:** the outcome of a prolonged period of food deprivation, often resulting in death.

**Subsistence farming:** a type of farming concerned with the production of items to satisfy the food and living requirements of farmers and their families. The emphasis is on self-sufficiency.

**Sustainable:** a term that describes actions and processes that minimise negative impacts on the environment and promote human well-being.

**Transnational corporation (TNC):** a large company operating in more than one country and typically involved in a range of economic activities.

**Undernutrition:** the condition that applies when people do not eat enough food.

# Websites

- **www.agribusinessaccountability.org** — views about the impacts of TNCs on food supply
- **www.drylandsresearch.org.uk** — good source of African case studies
- **www.fao.org** — principal website for information on all food and food security issues
- **www.ifpri.org** — International Food Policy Research Institute — an important site for information about famine and food security
- **www.practicalaction.org** — for details of appropriate technology schemes to combat food shortages
- **www.soilassociation.org** — information about organic farming

# Publications

- Millstone, M. & Lang, T. (2008) *The Atlas of Food*, Earthscan.
- Hill, M. (2002) *Arid and Semi-Arid Environments (Access to Geography)*, Hodder Education.
- Patel, R. (2007) *Stuffed and Starved: Markets, Power and the Hidden Battle for the World Food System*, Portobello.
- Tudge, C. (2007) *Feeding People is Easy*, Pari Publishing.

# Global patterns of food production and consumption

## Food production

Most of the global food supply is produced by agriculture in the form of arable crops and livestock. Water plays a lesser part through the sourcing of fish, crustaceans and seaweeds. It would be wrong to imagine that the graph of global **food production** has taken the form of a steadily rising curve. *Case study 1* makes the point that the incline of the graph has been broken by three significant steps or agricultural revolutions. The intriguing question is what, if anything, caused these breakthroughs? Trying to answer this question requires exploring the issue considered in Case Study 12, namely that between population and resources. Did the new technologies embodied in these revolutions just happen by chance? Or were they a response to a particular need, such as to produce more food to feed a surge in the global population?

---

| LEAPS IN FOOD PRODUCTION | 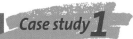 *Case study 1* |
| --- | --- |

### Three agricultural revolutions and the UK

The rise in global food production has not been a steady incremental process. History shows that there have been at least three giant leaps, all of which have been experienced in the UK. The advances have been so profound as to warrant the term 'revolution'.

### *Revolution 1 (circa 10 000 BC): the birth of farming*

Advances:

- Hunting and food-gathering give way to the domestication of a range of crops and livestock.
- Cereal farming (wheat, barley, millet, rice and maize) using the plough and draught animals.
- Cattle, sheep, goats and pigs reared for meat and milk, as well as for wool and hides.

Outcome:

- Farming of a sedentary, peasant kind becomes established and begins to spread from its cradle lands.

### Revolution 2 (1650–1850): the commercialisation of farming

Advances:
- New farming practices include crop rotation, improved varieties of root crops, and better maintenance of soil fertility through nitrogen-fixing plants and animal manure.
- More emphasis on livestock rearing.
- The Industrial Revolution greatly increases the demand for food and provides new modes of transport for the movement of food to growing urban markets.

Outcome:
- Food production becomes more market-oriented and is able to support a growing urban population.

### Revolution 3 (1930 to present): the industrialisation of farming

Advances:
- Farm mechanisation (the tractor, combine harvester, mechanical milking machines, factory farming).
- The use of **agrochemicals** (pesticides, herbicides, fungicides and artificial fertilisers).
- Food processing — agricultural produce undergoes more processing before reaching the consumer.
- Biotechnology and the genetic modification of crops, livestock and food.

Outcome:
- **Agribusiness** and the globalisation of food production.

There is no doubt that the UK played a leading part in launching Revolutions 2 and 3, but it is likely that Revolution 1 was first triggered elsewhere.

---

**1** **Using case studies**

**Try drawing a time line showing the three agricultural revolutions, and then suggest possible reasons for the long time break between Revolutions 1 and 2.**

**Guidance**

An arithmetic timescale will cause problems. There is a well established way round the problem — you need to use an alternative scale.

---

# Different food production systems

Today's population may be divided into two main groups: (1) those who produce their own food, and (2) those who rely on others to produce the food they need. This distinction marries up with that traditionally drawn between **subsistence farming** and **commercial farming**. Having said that, we need to remember that there is in fact a continuum running between these two types. For example, many so-called subsistence farmers will sell or trade any food that is surplus to their requirements. Equally, commercial farmers will consume some of the food that they produce.

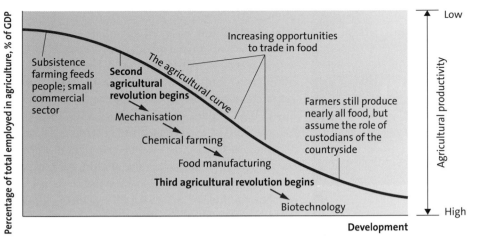

**Figure 1.1**
*The agricultural curve*

Another highly generalised view of the history of global food production is that there has been a significant shift from subsistence farming to commercial farming. While in some parts of the world, namely what the World Bank calls the low-income countries (LICs), the former continues to support significant numbers of people, the majority of today's global population relies on the latter. **Industrialisation** and urbanisation have been two key processes underlying this shift. The irony is that while the number of people to be fed continues to rise at an alarming rate, the trend in the agricultural curve has been downward (Figure 1.1). In most countries, agriculture's contribution to GDP and total employment continues to decline. The discrepancy is accounted for, of course, by the increasing productivity of farming, thanks particularly to the current agricultural revolution.

There is much concern today about the development gap that separates the wealthy states classified by the World Bank as high-income countries (HICs) from the struggling LICs. When it comes to narrowing that gap, two closely related strategies are widely advocated. The first is that the HICs should help the LICs by offering them appropriate aid. The second is that the world should encourage the economic development of LICs by involving them as active and equal partners in the global economy. A common component in both strategies is that LICs should become more involved in commercial agriculture. It is tempting to think that producing food for the affluent HIC market is one of a number of promising ways of closing the development gap. But some are beginning to question the wisdom of moving in this direction (*Case study 2*).

## SUBSISTENCE FARMING AND RURAL POVERTY

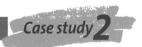

*Case study 2*

### Some myths dispelled

There are many who believe that subsistence farming is so closely associated with rural poverty and **famine** that it is to be regarded as a basic cause. As a consequence, they urge that rural communities should turn to commercial farming in order to break the vicious downward spiral. But the causes of poverty and famine are far more complex, as is well illustrated in the case of Kenya. The causal factors are environmental (land degradation, climate variability), economic (unemployment, low wages), demographic (impact

of HIV/AIDS), social (high costs of health and education), political (unrest, poor governance) and technological (low agricultural productivity — Figure 1.2).

One often-neglected snag with the conversion to commercial farming is that those involved have to eat. Instead of growing their own food, they have to buy it from others. In other words, they themselves become not just the producers of commercial food but also the consumers. So while involvement in commercial farming may promise regular paid work, much if not most of the associated income has to be spent on purchasing food. In most places, the price of basic food is notoriously high relative to wage levels. In Kenya over the last few years there has been a hike in the price of maize, the staple food crop. Prices have been driven by repeated periods of bad weather and a succession of poor harvests, as well as by the fact that the amount of land given over to maize has declined. That decline in crop area is partly explained by the conversion of some subsistence farmland to commercial cropland.

Another related problem is that for most people, turning to commercial farming means ceasing to be self-employed and becoming an employee. In other words, they can easily become pawns in the marketing struggles of agribusinesses. There is little security in terms of work and pay. Land that is lost to commercial farming is rarely if ever recovered for subsistence purposes.

The strengths of subsistence farming are rarely publicised. For example, it allows people to live in harmony with the environment and for this reason it is potentially much more **sustainable** than commercial farming. Besides its ecological appropriateness, other positives include its reliance on community cooperation, its local scale and its emphasis on self-reliance.

*In any effort to improve the quality of life of those who rely on subsistence farming it is important to preserve the positives indicated in this case study, as well as to seek out the real causes of rural poverty and famine. There is no quick and lasting fix to be found in commercial farming: it merely replaces one set of problems with another.*

**Figure 1.2**
*Kenya: rural poverty and subsistence farming — a causal link?*

Tom Uhlman/Alamy

Chris Howes/Wild Places Photography/Alamy

---

### Question

Using examples, identify and explain what you think are the positives of subsistence farming.

### Guidance

This question requires you to establish how secure subsistence farming is in terms of food production. This will also allow you to discuss any weaknesses in this context. Does subsistence farming have other positives outside food security? This should lead you to consider important aspects of quality of life other than food.

## COMMERCIAL FARMING AND HUNGER

### Villain or hero?

Many would argue that commercial food production emerged as part of the second agricultural revolution of the late eighteenth century, with Britain leading the way. To do so, however, would be to ignore at least two significant earlier developments. Networks of market towns have existed for centuries in many parts of the world. As trading points and centres of non-agricultural activities, they have relied heavily on the food surpluses produced by local farmers for sale or exchange. Later, and perhaps more overtly, there was the plantation system that European colonial powers developed in Africa, Asia and the Americas, starting in the early seventeenth century. The system persists to this day, with plantations producing then as now a range of highly commercial crops, from tea and coffee to cotton and rubber.

The achievements of commercial agriculture have been immense. It must be recognised that commercial food production, mainly operating as part of a capitalist system, has managed to feed the great majority of people in rapidly expanding populations. That in itself has been a considerable achievement and contrasts with what you will read in *Case study 5*. Without commercial food production, urbanisation and industrialisation would not have been sustained. True, there has always been an undernourished and hungry minority in the world, and there are some who put the blame for this on commercial agriculture. Such critics point to the fact that commercial food production is driven by market demands and profit maximisation, as if these were inborn genetic defects. However, rather better-informed critics are beginning to point to four recent developments in global agriculture that are perhaps to be blamed for unduly rising food prices and food shortages in poorer parts of the world (Figure 1.3). We shall return to this issue later in the book (*Case study 48*). At this stage it will suffice briefly to draw attention to four possible contributors:

- **The industrialisation of agriculture** — globally, agriculture has become more large-scale and more reliant on modern technology. Industrialised agriculture relies more on energy resources, especially oil. It is geared towards serving the world market and the export of food. It also involves the **outsourcing** of food production to LICs, taking advantage of cheap land and cheap labour. This important issue is explored in *Case study 48*.
- **The restructuring of agriculture in LICs** — countries have been forced to shift much of their food production away from subsistence crops to high-value exports (*Case study 2*). They have been pressured by the IMF and the World Bank to open up their markets to cheap food imports. As a result, local food production for domestic **consumption** has been undercut. The price of imported food has gone way up at the same time that the ability to produce food for local consumption has been eroded. This dual pressure has left millions of peasants and farmers no longer able to live off the land. It is these people who are flooding into the slums and shanty towns of the cities.
- **The production of biofuels** from sugar-rich crops such as maize, wheat and sugar cane has become a booming and very profitable industry. This means that land previously used for the production of food for human consumption is now being used for non-food agriculture (*Case studies 46 and 47*).

## Part 2

- **Financial speculation in food commodities** — just as in other sectors of economic activity, speculators buy, sell and hoard supplies of food. There are those who wheel and deal in future supplies of food. This involves entering into contracts for the delivery and sale of food that has not yet been produced. The claim is that this speculation drives up food prices (*Case study 43*).

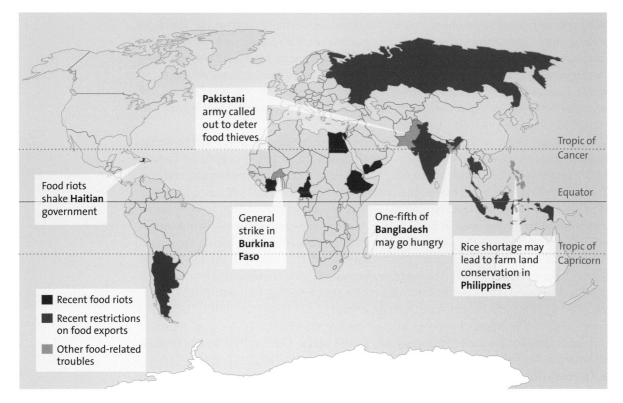

**Figure 1.3**
**Food shortages around the world:** *according to the World Bank, food prices have increased by 83% in the last 3 years*

*This case study makes the following points:*
- *Food production in the capitalist world is not solely the outcome of commercial agriculture.*
- *In many capitalist countries, the free play of market forces is constrained by various forms of government intervention.*
- *Globalisation of food production is being promoted by huge agribusinesses and blamed for increasing food prices and shortages in the developing world.*

### Question
What opportunities are there for developing economic activities in LICs outside commercial agriculture?

### Guidance
This question is best addressed if your answer focuses on one specific country. Consider other possible activities in the primary sector, as well as the secondary and tertiary sectors. You might also argue that commercial agriculture can provide opportunities as long as it remains in the hands of local producers and not agribusinesses.

There are many different types of farming system (Figure 1.4). They may be distinguished on the basis of a range of criteria, such as environment (equatorial → cold temperate; lowland → upland), location (shifting → sedentary), inputs (intensive → extensive), outputs (arable → pastoral), tenure (owner-occupied → tenancy → communal), government (capitalist → socialist) and market (subsistence → commercial). Remember that these criteria are not mutually exclusive. Any one agricultural system may be checked off against seven criteria. For example, a cereal farm in East Anglia may be classified as temperate, lowland, sedentary, owned by a company, arable, capitalist and commercial. All these criteria are factors that affect agriculture and the production of food in various ways, both direct and indirect.

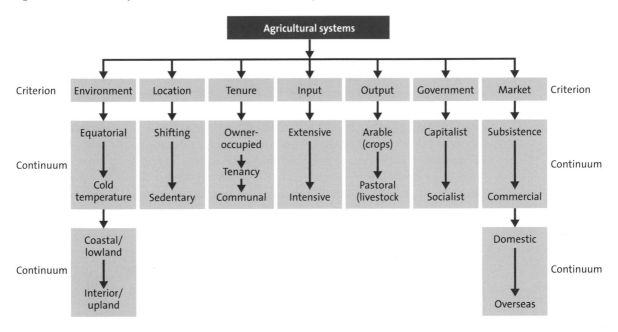

Figure 1.4 suggests one simple classification that will be followed throughout this book based on the government criterion. The prime distinction here is between the food production systems of the capitalist and socialist worlds. The two case studies that follow provide information that will allow you to compare the two systems.

*Figure 1.4*
*Classifying*
*agricultural systems*

## FOOD PRODUCTION IN THE CAPITALIST WORLD

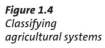
*Case study* **4**

### Another myth to dispel

The popular perception of farming in today's capitalist world is that it is all about big business, modern technology, the mass production of food and free market forces. This is true to only a limited extent in that even in the world's leading capitalist economies:

■ much of the food production remains in the hands of family farms rather than agribusinesses
■ there is still a significant amount of essentially subsistence farming
■ there is a considerable amount of government intervention, as in the EU and USA, in terms of deciding what farms produce and protecting home producers from overseas competition

The last point is particularly noteworthy. Take the example of the biggest and perhaps the most 'free' of all the capitalist economies, the USA. The greatest and one of the earliest government interventions in the history of US farming came in the form of the New Deal, designed to help farms recover from the devastating effects of the Great Depression. This included raising the prices paid for crops and livestock products as well as help with the conservation of soil resources. Following the Second World War, the federal government again stepped in. This time it was to reduce the surpluses resulting from the greatly increased agricultural productivity following farm mechanisation, plant and animal breeding and the application of chemical fertilisers. It did this by lowering commodity prices. But this was only part of a broader policy to increase demand and reduce supply and tackle broader issues such as poverty (**malnutrition**) and the conservation of soils exhausted by overexploitation.

Over the last few decades, economic globalisation has presented the US farm industry with some new challenges. Competition from new foreign food producers is threatening the 20–30% of US farm income derived from food exports. Rising imports of cheap food are not only putting farm livelihoods at risk but also raising trade tensions. The US government has become much more protective of its farming industry, curbing imports and supporting the prices of domestic products. There are also concerns about the safety of imported foods. This is part of a wider debate in the USA about **food consumption** (nutrition and balanced **diet**), food variety and bringing environmentally friendly production methods to food production. Figure 1.5 shows the degree of US government intervention in support of three aspects of food production — food and nutrition, conservation, and payments to farmers. Clearly, the first has become the major target.

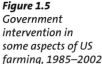

*Figure 1.5*
*Government intervention in some aspects of US farming, 1985–2002*

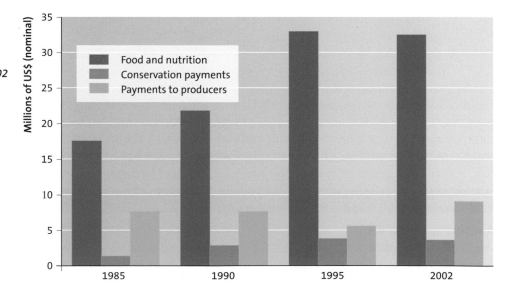

*The point to be stressed is that the USA is not the only capitalist economy in which food production is subject to government intervention. In Japan and the EU, the degree of intervention in the form of production quotas, subsidies and tariffs has possibly been even greater.*

# FOOD PRODUCTION IN THE SOCIALIST WORLD

## A tale of U-turns

The **collective**, an agricultural production unit made up of a number of farming households or villages working together under state control, has been a key feature of food production in the communist world. It was adopted in the Soviet Union in 1927 to encourage greater food production while freeing labour and capital for industrial development (Figure 1.6). By 1971 half the cultivated land in the Soviet Union was in collectives; most of the rest was in state farms. Neither in fact gave the country **food security**: food shortages and rationing were commonplace. With the collapse of communism in the early 1990s, it was hardly surprising that the majority of the Soviet collectives and state farms chose to privatise and register as agricultural companies operating in an emerging free-market situation.

Compared with the Soviet collective, the Chinese commune includes a wider range of activities (including non-agricultural ones) and puts greater emphasis on communal living. Collectivisation in China began in 1955, but it was not until 1958 that the cooperatives were merged into communes. Each commune would involve 20 to 30 cooperatives and 40 to 100 villages. Living communally, workers performed both industrial and agricultural tasks and supported a military unit. They used communal childcare, bathing and other facilities. Wages were controlled by the state, and all products were marketed through state agencies. However, the system failed to free the labour and capital needed for the industrialisation of China. Equally, the system did a poor job in feeding the people.

China is still a communist country, despite its recent moves towards a market economy, but the communes have been divided into private farms which are leased to farming families for 30 years. The farms pay a fixed amount of their produce to the state, and consume or sell the remainder. Chinese farmers are now able to hire labour, own machinery and, within limits, make their own farming decisions. The food situation has improved, but the country still suffers from **food insecurity**. Some farmland is now being leased to pharmaceutical companies and to capitalist-style enterprises such as the dairy farms in the Shanghai area.

Since the early 1990s the communist world, together with its farming system, has shrunk to a small fraction of its former self. Two tiny relicts survive in North Korea (*Case study 19*) and Cuba (*Case study 38*). Nearly all communist countries that have tried **collective farming** have found it wanting and made some sort of U-turn. One notable exception is North Korea. It has stuck steadfastly to the socialist model. The prevalence of malnutrition and **starvation** highlights the basic inability of the system adequately to feed the people. The situation is made worse by an autocratic government that is accused of being more interested in squandering resources on armaments than in safeguarding the health of its people.

TopFoto

***Figure 1.6***
*Soviet propaganda poster proclaiming the advances of collective farming*

*This case study makes the point that a number of Second World countries have tried a system of food production based on socialist principles. But in no instance has it proved capable of adequately feeding the people. Not surprisingly, there have been varying degrees of retreat towards more a more market-oriented mode of food production.*

**4**

*Using case studies*

## Question

**Identify ways in which food production in the capitalist world differs from that in the socialist world.**

## Guidance

You might work under the following headings: government intervention, land tenure, social conditions, efficiency and productivity.

# Global food production

Given the diversity of food that is produced around the world, the different systems involved in its production and the dearth of statistics in many parts, it is impossible to compile a reliable map of global food production. The best we can do is to look at some surrogate measures.

Perhaps the most obvious is per capita food production. Figure 1.7 looks at the situation in four of the world's developing regions. The trends suggest that Africa south of the Sahara is the only region where food production has not kept pace with the increase in population. The situation has been marginally better in the Near East and in north Africa. In the other two regions, there appears to have been a healthy increase in food production.

Global food production is conditioned by a range of physical and human factors. Those factors can have a positive or negative impact on output. Their significance will be illustrated in various subsequent case studies.

**Figure 1.7**
*Per capita food production in four developing regions, 1970–2005 (1970 = 100)*

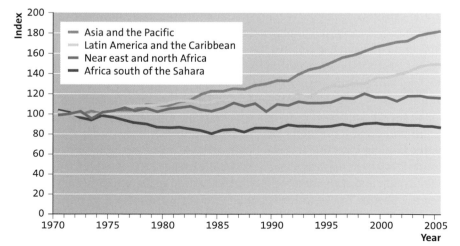

Legend:
- Asia and the Pacific
- Latin America and the Caribbean
- Near east and north Africa
- Africa south of the Sahara

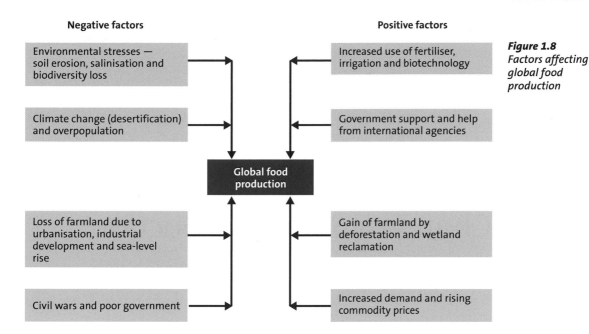

**Negative factors**

Environmental stresses — soil erosion, salinisation and biodiversity loss

Climate change (desertification) and overpopulation

Loss of farmland due to urbanisation, industrial development and sea-level rise

Civil wars and poor government

**Positive factors**

Increased use of fertiliser, irrigation and biotechnology

Government support and help from international agencies

Gain of farmland by deforestation and wetland reclamation

Increased demand and rising commodity prices

**Global food production**

*Figure 1.8*
*Factors affecting global food production*

Agricultural production, in terms of both its quantity and composition, is conditioned by a range of physical and human factors (Figure 1.8). A number of those factors are also used as criteria in the classification of agricultural systems. Another significant factor is the degree to which a national economy depends on agriculture (Figure 1.9).

*Figure 1.9*
*Agricultural output as percentage of GDP, 2000*

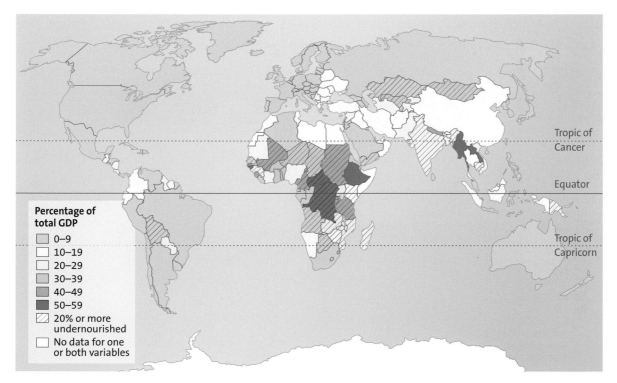

Percentage of total GDP
- 0–9
- 10–19
- 20–29
- 30–39
- 40–49
- 50–59
- 20% or more undernourished
- No data for one or both variables

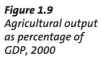

**Question**

Write an account that analyses the distribution shown by Figure 1.9.

**Guidance**

Start by describing the outstanding feature of the distribution — i.e. the dominance of countries where the proportion of GDP derived from agriculture is less than 20%. What types of country fall in this category? How do you explain the low values? Then move on to identify those areas where countries show a percentage value greater than say 40%. What types of country are they? Again, how do you explain the high values? What is the significance of the 20% or more undernourished?

# Changes in food production

Greater productivity is just one aspect of how food production changes over time (Figure 1.10). The relentless growth in the global population means more mouths to feed and hopefully the production of more food. There are also other significant changes over time, including:

■ the modes of food production, i.e. how the food is produced
■ the type of food that is produced

*Figure 1.10
Food production
change, 1990–2002*

Thanks to advances in technology such as mechanisation, plant and livestock breeding and the application of chemicals (fertilisers, pesticides, drugs etc.), much of the rising output of food in more developed countries comes from large-scale

farming operations that are run along business lines. In less developed countries, more food is produced as a result of the advances that made up the so-called **Green Revolution**.

**6**

**Using case studies**

Compare the distributions shown by Figures 1.9 and 1.10. What links can you identify?

**Guidance**

Try to match up the high- and low-value areas on both maps. This should then help you to make some links.

A number of factors encourage change in the type of food produced. It is known that with economic development, not only do people eat more, but also what they eat changes. Most notable is the rise in the consumption of meat and livestock products. The increased personal wealth that comes with economic development also gives people much greater freedom of choice concerning what they eat. The choice may be to eat only organic foods or fast foods.

Millions of people make these choices, and so both of these factors have an impact on what farmers are encouraged to produce. In HICs, while livestock rearing is a major branch of farming, organic farming is currently booming. So we begin to see the link between food production and food consumption. The demand patterns of the latter strongly influence what is produced.

## CHANGING TASTES IN CHINA

*Case study 6*

### Impacts on food production and health

In the 1960s, the Chinese diet was typically composed of rice, wheat, starchy roots and vegetables. Over the last two decades, however, the Chinese, particularly urban people, have dramatically increased their consumption of meat and other livestock products, and reduced their consumption of grain-based foods. Table 1.1 illustrates some significant shifts in the Chinese diet between the 1960s and the turn of the millennium. Clearly, these significant changes in food consumption patterns must be having an impact, if not on Chinese farming, then somewhere else in the world.

A prime cause of this change in the pattern of food consumption has been the considerable rise in personal wealth produced by China's booming economy and the high rate of urbanisation. Three other factors have also contributed:

**Table 1.1**
*Changes in the Chinese diet, 1960–2000*

| Consumption (per person) | Change (1960–2000) |
| --- | --- |
| Daily calorie supply | + 42% |
| Meat | × 4 |
| Other animal products | × 3 |
| Fruit and vegetables | × 5 |
| Fish | × 4 |
| Sweeteners | × 5 |
| Alcohol | × 7 |

- the gradual privatisation of food production since 1981 (*Case study 5*)
- the gradual elimination of food rationing in urban areas since 1981
- the opening of China's food processing to foreign direct investment

The first two factors have combined to allow Chinese agriculture to help meet the needs created by the changing urban diet. The last factor has opened the door to food imports, particularly from the USA. This is reinforced by the perception in urban China that it is 'cool' to eat Western foods.

Sadly, while these changes make urban **hunger** a thing of the past and allow Chinese food producers to benefit from the high prices now being paid for food, the fact that people are eating more and eating the wrong imported foodstuffs (fats, sugars and alcohol) creates a cost in terms of rising **obesity** and other health risks such as heart disease and diabetes.

*Economic development and increased personal wealth have given the residents of China's cities the chance to change their diets. This may be good news for China's farmers and foreign food producers, but it promises an unhealthy future for many city dwellers.*

# Food consumption

The link between food production and food consumption is achieved by the food supply chain. In HICs it takes the form shown in Figure 1 (page vi); in LICs the chain is simpler.

Food production and consumption are also linked by macro-scale factors. For example, as shown in *Case study 6*, the link is conditioned by economic development. But much more important are population numbers. We all need a certain amount of food each day in order to survive. That food requirement is expressed in terms of **daily calorie intake per person**. The precise figure depends on our age, gender, stature and activity levels, as well as climate. Table 1.2 shows how age and gender affect calorie intake requirements in the UK.

**Table 1.2** *Estimated average energy requirements, assuming low activity levels at work and leisure (kcal per day)*

| Age | Males | Females |
|---|---|---|
| 15–18 years | 2755 | 2110 |
| 19–49 years | 2550 | 1940 |
| 50–59 years | 2550 | 1900 |
| 60–64 years | 2380 | 1900 |
| 65–74 years | 2330 | 1900 |
| Over 75 years | 2100 | 1810 |

A map based on national mean daily calorie intake can give us a general impression of the global distribution of food consumption (Figure 1.11). What stand out are the high levels of consumption in North America, Europe, parts of north Africa and the Middle East, Australia and New Zealand. At the other extreme, our eye is drawn to low levels of consumption over much of Africa and in the central Asian country of Mongolia.

Daily calorie intake per person provides us with a scale along which we can mark certain critical thresholds in the human condition. This is sometimes referred to as the nutrition spectrum. It runs from starvation through to obesity. Critical conditions may be recognised along it (Figure 1.12):

■ **Undernutrition** occurs when the daily calorie intake falls slightly below the normal requirement. Hunger is a symptom.
■ **Malnutrition** literally means 'bad feeding' and is caused by an imbalance between what a person eats and what is needed to maintain good health. While it often results from eating too little, it can also be caused by an incorrect mix of protein, fat, carbohydrates, minerals and vitamins in the diet.

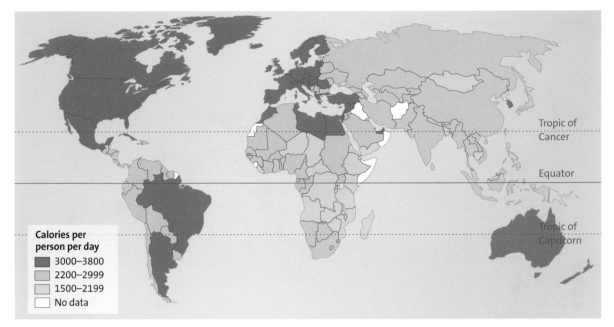

- **Hunger** results from an inadequate intake of food (undernutrition). Over a period of a few days, it is not health-threatening, but the longer it persists (i.e. becomes chronic) the greater is the likelihood of it leading to starvation and even death.
- **Starvation** is the outcome of a prolonged period of food deprivation (famine). It is the stage when hunger becomes so acute that it leads directly and often rapidly to death.

*Figure 1.11*
*The global distribution of daily calorie intake per person*

Further along the spectrum in the opposite direction (Figure 1.12) there are two critical conditions:

- **Overnutrition** is the condition in which food nutrients are oversupplied in relation to the amounts required for normal growth, development and metabolism. Some regard it as a form of malnutrition.
- **Obesity** is a medical condition in which excess body fat has accumulated to the extent that it may have an adverse effect on health, leading to reduced life expectancy. The body mass index (BMI), which compares weight and height, is used to define a person as overweight (pre-obese) when it is between $25\,\mathrm{kg\,m^{-2}}$ and $30\,\mathrm{kg\,m^{-2}}$ and obese when it is greater than $30\,\mathrm{kg\,m^{-2}}$. Obesity is most commonly caused by a combination of excessive dietary calories, lack of physical activity, and genetic susceptibility. It is associated with many diseases, particularly heart disease, Type 2 diabetes, breathing difficulties, certain types of cancer and osteoarthritis.

*Figure 1.12*
*The nutrition spectrum*

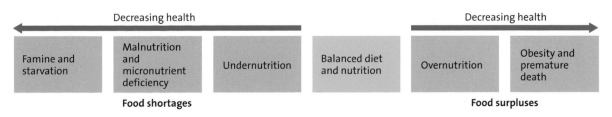

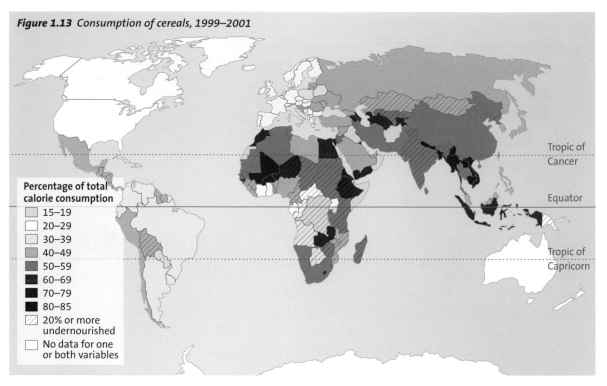

**Figure 1.13** *Consumption of cereals, 1999–2001*

**Percentage of total calorie consumption**
- 15–19
- 20–29
- 30–39
- 40–49
- 50–59
- 60–69
- 70–79
- 80–85
- 20% or more undernourished
- No data for one or both variables

Tropic of Cancer

Equator

Tropic of Capricorn

Figures 1.13 and 1.14 illustrate the fundamental difference between the developed and developing worlds in terms of food consumption and diets.

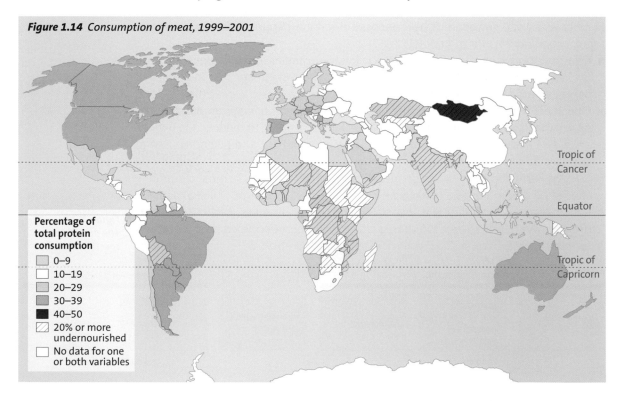

**Figure 1.14** *Consumption of meat, 1999–2001*

**Percentage of total protein consumption**
- 0–9
- 10–19
- 20–29
- 30–39
- 40–50
- 20% or more undernourished
- No data for one or both variables

Tropic of Cancer

Equator

Tropic of Capricorn

## Question

Compare Figures 1.13 and 1.14. Are there areas where the consumption of cereals and that of meat seem to be fairly balanced?

## Guidance

Identify the countries that show middle-range values in both maps.

## MALNUTRITION IN ETHIOPIA

*Case study 7*

### A persistent 'epidemic'

With daily calorie intake averaging 1540 calories per day per person, around 8 million people out of Ethiopia's total population of 82 million rely on food aid in order to survive. But rising levels of severe acute malnutrition are expected to increase that dependency still further. Those most at risk are children under the age of 5. Infant mortality currently stands at 156 per 1000 live births — one of the highest rates in the world.

The factors contributing to this malnutrition 'epidemic' are environmental, demographic and economic:

- Population densities are high in relation to food resources. The overall population density is 72 people per km$^2$.
- Climate variability leaves farming highly dependent on the rainy seasons: the main one is from June to September, with a lesser one from February to April. In good years, the latter allows farmers to produce a second crop. In recent years, both seasons have failed to produce sufficient rainfall.
- Widespread poverty means that many families simply do not have the means to buy food, particularly during times of crop failure.
- Rising global costs of fuel, fertiliser and staple foods are compounding the problem, especially for the poorest Ethiopians. The price of maize and sorghum has doubled within a year, while the price of wheat has increased by more than half.

The vulnerability of children to malnutrition is explained by a complex interaction of factors such as the mother's health and diet during pregnancy and her knowledge of basic nutrition, as well as poor-quality water supply and sewage disposal.

*It is difficult to see any long-term solution to this humanitarian crisis in Ethiopia and other areas in the Horn of Africa. Possible actions include large-scale water conservation projects, the development of food production methods, the introduction of crops and livestock better adapted to the increasingly arid conditions, and perhaps population control. The only option in the short term is to rely on food aid provided by the international community.*

## Question

Which of the causes of malnutrition in Ethiopia do you think are capable of being relieved? Give your reasons.

## Guidance

Distinguish those causes that lie outside Ethiopia's control and then look more closely at the remainder.

### Case study 8 · GLOBESITY STRIKES THE UK

#### A fast route to premature death

There have always been fat people, and it has long been known that the incidence of obese (body mass index [BMI] of more than $30\,kg\,m^{-2}$) and overweight (BMI of more than $24.9\,kg\,m^{-2}$) people in a population increases with the general rise in the standard of living. It also increases with age. For example, the number of people in England aged 55–64 who are overweight or obese is more than double the number aged 16–24. But the alarm bells are ringing in the UK because the percentage of adults who are obese has roughly doubled since the mid-1980s. Daily calorie intake in the UK has now risen to 3190 calories per person per day (Figure 1.15).

Genetic factors account for a proportion of cases of obesity, but the recent and sudden surge in weight levels (referred to as **globesity** since it is so widespread) can only be explained by environmental factors. Eating too many calories for our energy needs is a major candidate for the main cause of the current obesity epidemic. The type of food eaten is also playing an important role. Researchers are discovering more metabolic and digestive disorders resulting from overconsumption of fats and refined white

*Figure 1.15*
*Overweight children at a weight-loss centre in Leeds*

Homer W. Sykes/Alamy

flour combined with a low fibre intake. Increases in the consumption of calorie-rich foods, as evidenced by the growth of fast-food chains and higher soft drink consumption, also add to the energy surplus that leads to obesity. The problem is made worse by the small amount of exercise that figures in modern lifestyles, exercise being a potentially effective burner of excess calories.

The outcome of obesity is a range of increased health risks, from Type 2 diabetes to heart disease, from strokes to colon cancer. The alarming truth is that increasing numbers of us are literally eating our way to an early grave. Also alarming is that a lack of self-confidence and of pride in appearance may be contributing to the obesity.

*Our modern lifestyles are major contributors to the obesity epidemic — we are eating too much, our diet includes too much of the wrong foods and we are taking too little exercise.*

## Using case studies

### 9

**Conduct a survey in your local shopping centre and calculate the percentages of those passing by who you think are (a) overweight, and (b) obese.**

### Guidance

You need to think how best to conduct your survey, particularly the sampling strategy. Perhaps it will suffice to carry out the survey over three specified time periods on the same day.

The conclusion to be drawn from *Case studies 7 and 8* is that the extremes of the daily calorie intake continuum are both life-threatening, but in rather different ways. Both conditions result principally from what are described as 'environmental' factors. In the case of malnutrition, it is the physical environment. With overnutrition, it is the human environment of lifestyles and levels of affluence.

# Global patterns of food security and insecurity

## The state of food security

In the previous section we looked separately at the global patterns of food production and food consumption. We now focus on the critical relationship between them. It is this relationship that determines a key aspect of the human condition — food security. **Food security** exists where people do not go hungry or live in fear of starvation. They have access to sufficient food to enable them to lead a healthy life. In other words, it prevails where food supply meets the demand for food (i.e. food production equals or exceeds food consumption). What needs to be understood, however, is that in order for a country or region to have food security, it does not necessarily have to produce itself all the food needed to feed its people. Food security can also be achieved by supplementing domestic production with imported food. Of course, reliance on food imports requires that the country or region has the means (either capital or goods) to acquire that food. It also goes without saying that the level of food security is greater where a country or region produces all its food rather than having to rely on imported supplies. Trade can so easily be disrupted by changing economic and political circumstances.

Food security involves rather more than the simple availability of food. At household level, food can only be bought if it is sold at prices that people can afford. Equally, it is possible that there may be sufficient food available within a country or region, but access to it requires adequate transport and storage facilities, as well as effective marketing or retailing networks.

So which countries in today's world are the most food-secure? Would we be right in thinking that the most secure are the leading HICs? The following case study comes up with a surprising answer.

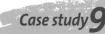 **Case study 9** — WHICH ARE THE MOST FOOD-SECURE NATIONS?

### Some surprises

To ask which countries in the world are the most food-secure may seem a rather academic question with an obvious answer. Understandably, we are more interested in the question of food insecurity, if only for humanitarian reasons and the sense that

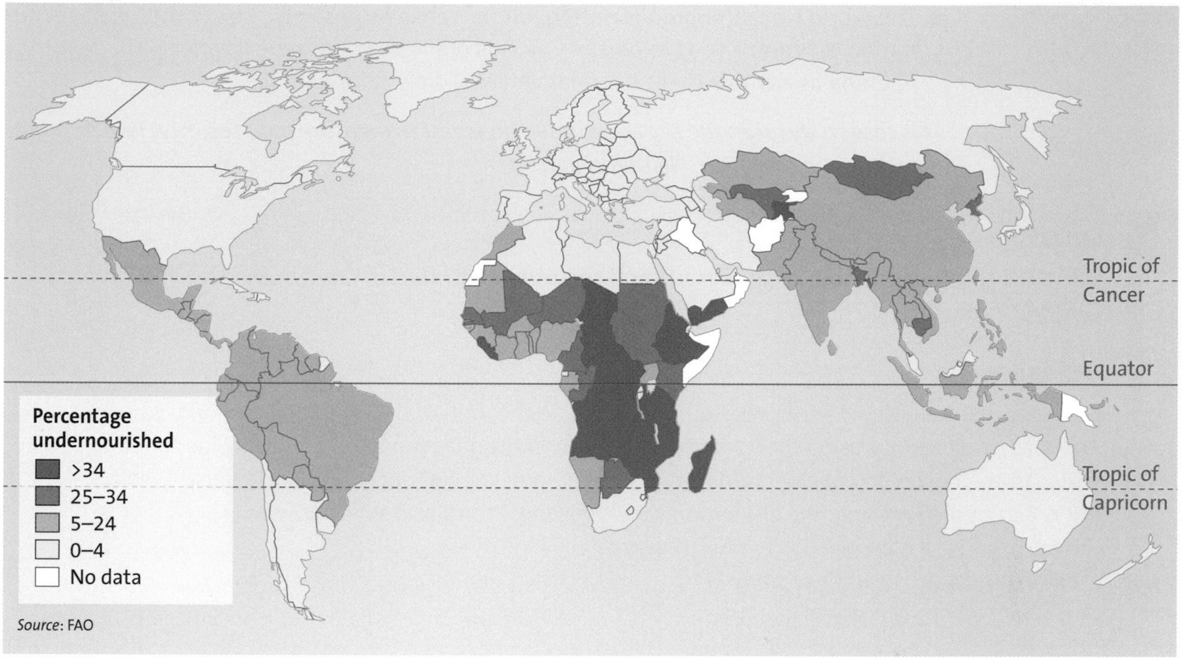

**Figure 2.1**
*Global distribution of undernourishment, 2003–05*

Percentage undernourished
- >34
- 25–34
- 5–24
- 0–4
- No data

*Source*: FAO

the elimination of **food insecurity** is a challenge requiring immediate action. A look at Figure 2.1 might provide an answer to the question, in that it is reasonable to argue that food security is greatest in those countries where the incidence of undernourishment is least. As might have been expected, the HICs dominate the low-value areas, but not completely: the leading HICs are importers of food — for example, 15% of Japan's imports are food, while for the UK the figure is 8%. The map also shows countries in north Africa, the Middle East, southeast Asia and South America which lie outside the HIC category.

So perhaps there is an alternative and possibly better indicator of food security. One such might be the degree to which a country produces all the food it consumes. In other words, the security lies in not having to rely on food produced in other countries and its associated risks. Unfortunately there are no international data about the degree to which countries are self-sufficient in terms of food supply. However, there are data about food imports, and so the percentage importance of foodstuffs in a country's total imports might be used as a surrogate measure.

Table 2.1 lists the top ten countries with the smallest percentage of imports of food and livestock. Data are also given for exports. What do we find?

- Three of the countries — Turkey, Australia and Thailand — also appear to be significant exporters of food. In other words, they have surplus food to dispose of.
- Four of the countries — Singapore, Malaysia, Taiwan and South Korea — are NICs known as the 'Asian Tigers', which have achieved their developmental status largely thanks to manufacturing and services.

**Table 2.1**
*The top ten most food-secure countries (2000)*

| Country | Food and livestock | |
|---|---|---|
| | % of all imports by value | % of all exports by value |
| Turkey | 2.0 | 18.2 |
| China | 2.7 | 8.3 |
| Singapore | 3.3 | 2.4 |
| Australia | 3.6 | 13.2 |
| Thailand | 3.7 | 20.6 |
| South Africa | 4.0 | 5.7 |
| Malaysia | 4.3 | 2.9 |
| Taiwan | 4.5 | 0.9 |
| South Korea | 4.6 | 2.4 |
| Austria | 4.8 | 2.9 |

- The world's most populous nation, China, ranks as possibly the second most secure nation. It is also a food exporter. Can this really be so? Maybe it reflects the fact that in China as a whole there is a relatively low daily calorie intake.

*This case study raises the key question — how best to measure food security. Two different measures are used here. Neither is perfect.*

**10** **Question**

**Which of the two possible measures of food security illustrated in *Case study 9* do you favour? Give your reasons.**

**Guidance**

Neither provides a direct measure. Both provide an indication of the aggregate national situation. The reasoning behind using the trade measure is perhaps questionable; also, reliability of data varies from country to country. Undernourishment involves standardised data collected by the FAO. You might conclude the discussion by suggesting a third and superior measure — that is, provided you are convinced you have a 'winner'.

Before you start, read *Case study 10*.

It is probably true to say that it is in the best interests of every nation to produce as much of its own food as possible. Any dependence on food from foreign sources carries with it a strategic risk that these supplies might suddenly and without warning be cut off. It is highly likely that over the centuries many wars over territory have also had the aim of securing additional food supplies.

Two more observations should be made about food security:
- It provides the context for the '**feast**' (sumptuous eating) that figures in some of the GCE geography specifications. But the 'feast' can have some unwanted consequences, such as wasting food, eating too much and eating an ill-balanced diet (*Case study 8*).
- Countries that may be regarded as food-secure at an aggregate level often have within their populations groups which do not enjoy that status. This is true even in some of the world's richest countries, including the USA.

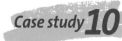 **Case study 10** THE UNUSUAL CASE OF SINGAPORE

### Is it really food-secure?

According to Table 2.1 the small state of Singapore is one of the most food-secure countries in the world. The Republic of Singapore came into being in 1965, since when it has become one of the world's wealthiest nations. The development of Singapore is all the more remarkable considering its small size (622 km$^2$) and small population (4.7 million). Added to that is the fact that it has to import virtually all its water, energy and industrial raw materials, and most of its food. Agriculture's contribution to the economy is less than 1% of GDP. Singapore's agriculture only produces vegetables, poultry, eggs and fish. Virtually all of its staple food, rice, is imported.

RICO/Fotolia

*Figure 2.2*
*Singapore — a*
*dynamic city state*

By now you will be looking back at Table 2.1 and asking how is it that food imports account for such a small percentage of total imports. The answer is that Singapore's imports include large quantities of much more costly commodities, such as oil and industrial raw materials. You might also ask how is it that Singapore also exports 'food and livestock'. The answer is that it exports two commodities — orchids and ornamental fish — that happen to be classified under this heading.

Singapore looks very food-secure so long as the secondary, tertiary and quaternary sectors of its economy are booming (Figure 2.2). By Singapore standards, imported food is very cheap. But what would happen if Singapore fell out with its immediate neighbour Malaysia and the country was blockaded? Food security would quickly turn to insecurity.

*To ensure food security, a country cannot do better than to produce all its own food.*

**11**

**Using case studies**

### Question

Give some specific examples of food-insecure areas within food-secure countries. You might research one of the following countries: Australia, South Africa or the USA.

### Guidance

Remember that food insecurity and poverty often go hand in glove, that prosperous countries have their lagging or peripheral regions, and that deprivation exists within cities.

# Food insecurity and its causes

One of the ironies of the modern world is that there is no overall shortage of food and yet there is much hunger and often famine. In short, at both an individual and national level there is food insecurity, and it seems to be on the increase. Food insecurity may be defined as a situation in which there is a high risk of hunger and famine. There are a number of possible indicators of food insecurity at the national level. One favoured by the UN Food and Agriculture Organization (FAO) is the incidence of undernourishment (*Case study 9*).

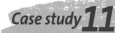

## THE NUMBER OF GLOBAL HUNGRY NEARS 1 BILLION

### The rise and spread of food insecurity

Figure 2.1 (page 21) provides a snapshot of global food insecurity in 2003–05 based on a survey by the FAO. This revealed that the vast majority of the world's undernourished people lived in developing countries, which were home to 832 million chronically hungry people. Since then, there is every indication that the figure has continued to rise. Driven by environmental disasters, rising food prices and civil wars, it now approaches 1 billion. Sixty-five per cent of these 'hungry' people live in only seven countries: India, China, the Democratic Republic of Congo, Bangladesh, Indonesia, Pakistan and Ethiopia. Progress in these countries with their large populations would obviously have an important impact on the overall food security situation and on any reduction of hunger in the world. China has made significant progress in reducing undernourishment following years of rapid economic growth.

The proportion of people who suffer from hunger in the total population remains highest in sub-Saharan Africa, where one in three people is chronically hungry. Latin America and the Caribbean were continuing to make good progress in hunger reduction

***Figure 2.3**
Countries facing
food crises, 2008*

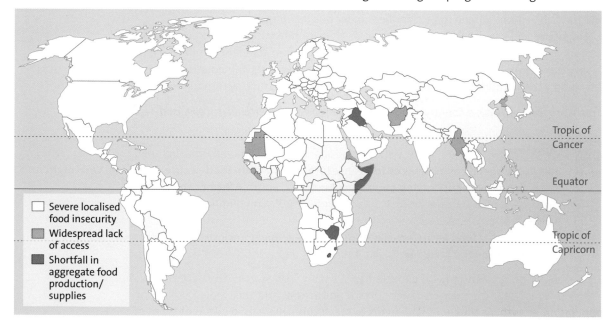

Severe localised food insecurity

Widespread lack of access

Shortfall in aggregate food production/supplies

Tropic of Cancer

Equator

Tropic of Capricorn

before the dramatic increase in food prices at the beginning of the millennium; together with east Asia and the Near East and north Africa, these regions maintain some of the lowest levels of undernourishment in the developing world.

Seven countries are shown in Figure 2.1 as having 'no data' — Western Sahara, Somalia, Muscat and Oman, Iraq, Afghanistan, Kyrgyzstan and Papua New Guinea. Is it a mere coincidence that these particular countries happen to be host to factors commonly associated with (if not causes of) food insecurity — namely harsh physical environments and political unrest?

Figure 2.3 provides an update by identifying the countries facing food crises in 2008, i.e. those that were arguably the most food-insecure. It confirms the direness of the situations in three of Figure 2.1's 'missing' countries (Afghanistan, Iraq and Somalia), where civil unrest is clearly a major causal factor.

*It is particularly worrying that rates of undernourishment are high in countries with large populations. Globally, sub-Saharan Africa stands out as a hunger hotspot. Political unrest appears to be a significant contributory cause.*

## 12 Question

**Suggest possible reasons for the apparent link between large populations and high rates of undernourishment.**

### Guidance

It is tempting to argue that large populations will always contain large numbers of undernourished people — an arithmetic fact. However, the situation is being portrayed in percentage terms. So it would be better to investigate possible reasons in terms of population densities, difficult natural environments, overpopulation and other causes, such as human wars.

Exploration of the reasons for food insecurity is best started in the wider context of the relationship between population and food supply. Too great a population pressure on resources, especially those that yield the supply of food, is widely recognised as leading most directly to food insecurity.

## POPULATION AND FOOD SUPPLY

Case study 12

### Some different views

**Malthus** (1798) based his view of the critical relationship between population and food supply on two principles:

- In the absence of any checks, human population has the potential to grow at a geometric rate (2, 4, 8, 16 and so on). In other words, population numbers can double within a generation (i.e. every 25 years).
- Even in the most favourable circumstances, food production can only be expected to increase at an arithmetic rate (1, 2, 3, 4 and so on).

Thus population growth may be expected to outstrip food supply. Furthermore, the ability of every country to produce food has a finite limit, and this sets a 'ceiling' on population growth. As a population begins to reach this ceiling, two different types of check come into play that stop or reduce population growth (Figure 2.4). Preventive checks include abstinence from, or delay in the timing of, marriage and pregnancy. This helps to reduce fertility rates. Positive checks include famine, disease, war and infanticide, all of which help to raise death rates.

**Boserup** (1965) based her view of the relationship on the argument that in an agricultural society, any increase in population stimulates an improvement in agricultural techniques, thus increasing food supply (Figure 2.4). In more advanced societies, the manufacture of goods and the provision of services allow food to be purchased from external sources.

**The Club of Rome** (1972) produced a report entitled *Limits to Growth*. This stated that if current trends in global population growth, industrialisation, food production and resource depletion continued unchanged, the absolute limit to global numbers would be reached sometime in the following 100 years. However, the report argued that it is still possible to alter these growth trends and to reach an equilibrium that is sustainable into the future. In the present circumstances, people have a choice. If they opt for the second scenario, the sooner they begin working to attain it, the greater will be the chances of human survival. However, the looming menace of global warming and its far-reaching repercussions are a warning that the Club of Rome's first option could so easily materialise.

**Neo-Malthusians** (1968 and later) argue that the current food shortages in some LICs are clear evidence of **overpopulation**. In other words, there are too many people for the resources available to feed them at current levels of technology. Paul Ehrlich

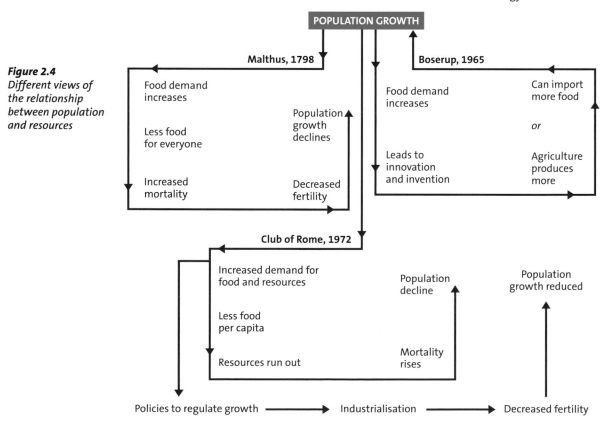

**Figure 2.4**
*Different views of the relationship between population and resources*

was an early proponent of this view in his book *The Population Bomb* (1968). Neo-Malthusians argue that the problem of food shortages will only be solved when population is controlled either by some ecological disaster (climate change or the exhaustion of non-renewable resources) or by a substantial reduction in the fertility rate (resulting, for example, from the HIV/AIDS pandemic). Their view accords with the Club of Rome model.

Currently, the rate of global population growth is beginning to slow. Some experts forecast that the global population will peak in 2030 (at 7.4 billion); others say this will happen in 2050 (at nearly 8.9 billion) and still others suggest 2070 (9.2 billion).

*There are contrasting views (both optimistic and pessimistic) about the balance between population and food supplies and what is likely to happen to this balance over the next 50 years. Will the rate of increase in the global food supply be outstripped by the rate of population growth?*

**13** **Question**

**Evaluate the different viewpoints on population pressure on food supplies.**

**Guidance**

1 Briefly explain what is meant by 'population pressure on food supplies'.
2 Summarise each of the different viewpoints in a few sentences.
3 Address two questions: which viewpoints are validated on the basis of what has happened in the past, and which viewpoints look like being the best predictors of what will happen to the population–food equation.
4 Nominate a 'winner' or attempt to rank the viewpoints in terms of their credibility.

*Using case studies*

Central to the discussion of the relationship between population and food supply is the concept of **carrying capacity** and the three states or conditions: overpopulation, underpopulation and optimum population. Carrying capacity is the maximum number of people that can be supported at a given standard of living by the resources and technology in a given area. Overpopulation occurs when this capacity is exceeded. Although a high density of population often accompanies overpopulation, it is not the same thing. The carrying capacity is perhaps more likely to be exceeded by a sudden surge in population numbers. With too many mouths to feed, food insecurity is almost bound to follow.

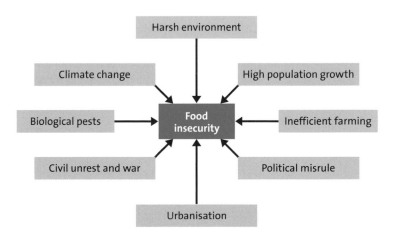

*Figure 2.5*
*Food insecurity: causal factors*

Figure 2.5 shows other factors than can contribute to food insecurity. These are explored and illustrated in the related case studies.

## Climate change

The history of the Earth is a story of climate change. The general consensus is that climate change is taking place today at a faster rate than at any time in human history. All manner of other changes in the world are now being laid at the door of climate change, particularly global warming. But in some instances, the assumed causal link is by no means certain. This is well illustrated by the process of **desertification**, which by reducing the agricultural productivity of large areas is undoubtedly responsible for increasing food insecurity in many parts of the world. The key question is this: is desertification the outcome of natural climate change or of human activities? (*Case study 35*)

## High population growth

The higher the population growth rate, the greater the chances are that the number of mouths to feed will outstrip available food supplies. In short, rapid population growth is often a fast route to food insecurity. A good example is provided by Ethiopia (*Case study 7*). Its population growth rate is 3.2%, the ninth fastest in the world. A population of 82 million means that Ethiopia has more than 2 million extra people to feed each year. With less than 20% of the population classified as urban and few exports, Ethiopia is very much an agrarian country and manifestly falling further and further behind in terms of raising its output of food. It is regarded by the FAO as facing a serious food crisis (Figure 2.3). It is hardly surprising that the incidence of malnutrition is rising.

### Civil unrest and war

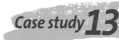 *Case study 13*

### DARFUR IS DYING

#### Civil war feeds food insecurity

Located on the southern edge of the Sahara and lying within the Sahel, Darfur (Sudan) at the best of times presents extremely difficult conditions for growing crops, raising livestock and living. Sixty per cent of the state's population of 1.4 million is constantly nagged by doubts as to whether the rains will come and whether they will have enough food to survive. When there is a good rainy season, farmers often lack the food processing and storage know-how to help overcome shortages during poor years.

NGOs have been working with poor communities living in environmentally fragile areas for many years to help improve their food security. Help has been focused on ways to improve food production and food processing. Sadly, these well intentioned efforts have been negated by a civil war that has plagued the state since 2003 following five consecutive years of drought (a possible indicator of climate change).

Initially, the civil war was between Arab and non-Arab, but now it is largely between two tribes, one comprising pastoralists and the other arable farmers. Nomadic herdsmen, escaping the areas worst hit by the prolonged drought and seeking water and pasture for their animals, have entered North Darfur and settled in what used to be a traditional crop-growing area with an adequate water supply. Supplies of water are inadequate to meet the needs of both tribes, while pasture can only be created by the acquisition of land previously given over to the cultivation of crops.

This war over water and farmland has badly damaged the infrastructure of Darfur — so much so that it has widened the gap between food supply and demand and increased food insecurity. Forty-five per cent of the population are now relying on emergency food aid. Malnutrition is on the rise; so too are deaths. In 2008 the UN estimated that during the 5-year civil war over 300 000 people had died (earlier estimates had claimed that 500 people were dying each day). Possibly one-third of those deaths were a direct result of the fighting and abuses of human rights. The remainder were due to starvation, disease and exposure. In addition, it has been estimated that 3 million people have been displaced by the conflict. By 2009, it seemed that the conflict might be beginning to abate as more peace-keeping troops arrived from other countries.

## Political misrule

| THE DEMISE OF FOOD SECURITY IN ZIMBABWE | Case study 14 |

### A tale of misrule and corruption

In the 1960s, when European rule in Africa was coming to an end, Southern Rhodesia (now Zimbabwe) was one of the most prosperous and food-secure parts of Africa. In 1965, the white government issued a unilateral declaration of independence from the UK, then its colonial master. In retaliation, the UK imposed trade sanctions that hit the country's economy. In 1980, the first multiracial elections were held and Robert Mugabe's ZANU PF party won. He became prime minister (later president) and soon established a one-party Marxist state. This marked the start of Zimbabwe's accelerating slide into food insecurity.

The once prosperous agricultural sector was a significant exporter of agricultural products such as tobacco and cotton. Today those exports have largely ceased. Indeed Zimbabwe can no longer produce sufficient food to feed its population. A particularly damaging political act was the so-called land reform, which forcibly dispossessed white farmers and redistributed their land among black Zimbabweans. This was thought to be a quick way of boosting support for the regime. However, much of the land was given to supporters close to Mugabe. To make the problem worse, most of those recipients had little interest in farming the land or putting it to good economic use.

Food production in Zimbabwe fell to such low levels and food insecurity became so acute that by 2008 roughly half of the country's population did not have access to an adequate food supply. Food shortages, empty shelves in supermarkets (Figure 2.6) and rampant inflation were clear signs that the country was on the brink of a humanitarian disaster.

So what caused this dramatic slide into food insecurity? Factors included a succession of poor harvests due to adverse weather. But more significant were:

■ inept agricultural policies, such as the land reform programme and the government's price controls on agricultural products
■ hyperinflation and a rapidly depreciating currency
■ a lack of key agricultural inputs such as fertilisers and tractors
■ the breakdown of irrigation systems through lack of maintenance
■ the debilitating effects of a high incidence of HIV/AIDS

But underlying all these factors was a corrupt government clinging to power by violence and ballot rigging.

**Figure 2.6**
*Empty supermarket shelves in Harare, Zimbabwe*

Mark Eveleigh/Alamy

The creation of a new coalition government in 2008, in which ZANU PF reluctantly agreed to share power with the opposition party, the Movement for Democratic Change, was seen as a possible move towards improvement. The early signs following this change were that the plunge into food insecurity might be starting to level off, although the continuing presence of Mugabe as head of state left prospects uncertain. While food began to return to the shelves of supermarkets, the shortfall in maize production of around 1.2 million tonnes in 2009 raised the number of people requiring food assistance past the 5 million mark.

## Rising food prices

A point about Figure 2.5 (see page 27) that needs to be stressed is that these individual causal factors also increase food insecurity by contributing to rising prices.

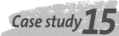

**Case study 15**   RISING FOOD PRICES

### Who is to blame?

Globally, the prices of food staples such as maize, wheat and rice are escalating (Figure 2.7). This suggests that demand is outstripping supply. But is that really so? Is the world really short of food?

It is claimed that there is enough food in the world today to feed 10 billion vegetarians. It is also claimed that increased Chinese prosperity and rising meat consumption are driving up cereal prices, because cereals are increasingly being diverted into livestock production. It takes about 8 kg of grain to produce 1 kg of beef, and 2.5 kg to produce 1 kg of poultry. As *Case study 6* illustrates, it is true that Chinese meat consumption is rising, but China has produced nearly all the extra grain it needs to support its growing numbers of livestock. Indeed, China is a net exporter of cereals. Chinese maize yields currently run at about 5 tonnes per hectare. This compares with

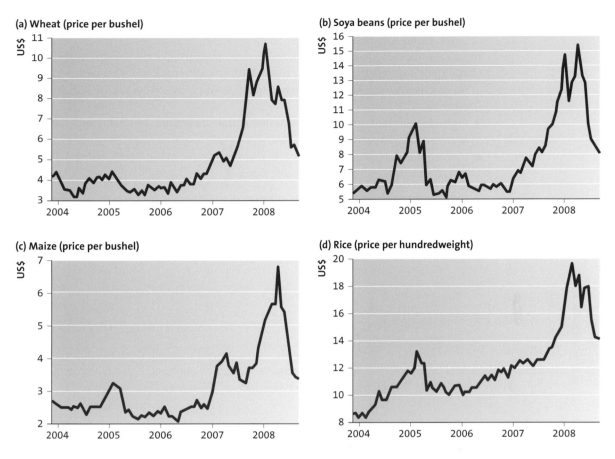

**(a) Wheat (price per bushel)**

**(b) Soya beans (price per bushel)**

**(c) Maize (price per bushel)**

**(d) Rice (price per hundredweight)**

US yields of about 9.4 tonnes per hectare. In short, Chinese yields could be nearly doubled using existing technologies.

*Figure 2.7*
*Rising food prices*

So what is driving up food prices? Many point the finger at high oil prices. These have made food production more expensive by raising the costs of mechanical cultivation, inputs such as fertilisers and pesticides, and the transport of both inputs and outputs. National policies to promote biofuels are diverting food production (maize, sugar cane, soya beans) into fuel production. Less food produced inevitably means higher prices. It is estimated that rising biofuel demand accounts for 30% of the increase in average cereal prices.

In response to higher food prices, several major food-producing countries have instituted export bans on various agricultural commodities. For example, China has banned rice and maize exports, and India has banned exports of rice and pulses. Argentina has raised export taxes on soya beans, maize, wheat and beef, and Ethiopia and Tanzania have banned exports of major cereals. Export controls shrink the size of the market and reduce the domestic prices paid to farmers. Price controls are especially damaging because they strongly discourage farmers from increasing their production. It has been claimed that the elimination of export bans would stabilise cereal price fluctuations, reduce price levels by as much as 30%, and enhance the efficiency of agricultural production. Eliminating subsidies for biofuel production in developed countries and export controls in developing countries would go a long way towards easing the world food crisis.

Finally, as a result of the 'credit crunch' that began in 2007, there have been cutbacks in agricultural research focused on boosting yields that might help LICs. LIC governments themselves have under-invested in farm-to-market roads and generally discouraged imports of fertiliser as well as high-yielding and genetically modified seeds.

Having read this, you might have spotted two possible ways of reducing food insecurity:

- Promote vegetarianism, particularly in the more developed countries with high levels of meat consumption.
- Discourage subsistence farmers in developing countries from being lured into commercial agriculture (*Case studies 2 and 3*).

You might also think of a third way — promoting **GM crops** (*Case study 36*, page 70).

*During the first decade of the twenty-first century, a marked rise in global food prices accelerated into a surge in 2008. It seems to have been due to a convergence of events, not least of which was the credit crunch.*

**14** **Using case studies**

### Question

**Analyse the graphs in Figure 2.7.**

### Guidance

The main task here is to identify and describe the trends. However, once you have done that, you might gain additional credit for offering some brief explanation of those trends.

**15** **Using case studies**

### Question

**Which of *Case studies 7, 13, 14, 15* and *35* do you think illustrates the most serious case of food insecurity?**

### Guidance

The nub of the question is — which of the different causes described is going to be most resistant to any corrective action? Might it be that those 'insecure' situations with human causes are likely to be more easily rectified than those created by natural forces? Producing a quadrant summary table may well help your answer.

It needs to be understood that food security varies not only from place to place, but also over time on both short- and long-term timescales. The increasing unreliability of weather and bouts of civil unrest are factors commonly underlying short-term phases of food insecurity, while in the long run overpopulation and global warming are likely to be serious causes.

One of the Millennium Development Goals (2000) is to free the world from hunger and to raise food security. Progress so far has been modest. Undoubtedly there are some countries in which food security has been increased, but many remain in need of improvement. Food security will continue to be a global concern for at least the next 50 years. Recently, crop yields have fallen in many areas because of declining investment in research and infrastructure, as well as increasing water scarcity. Climate change and HIV/AIDS are also crucial factors affecting food security in many parts of the world. The latter makes an impact through reducing the available labour supply. It is significant that even the more food-secure countries, such as the UK, are currently reappraising their food security in the light of likely global changes in the foreseeable future (*Case study 42*).

# Famine and life on the margins

## Food insecurity and famine

Food insecurity might be thought of as a sort of 'water-table' lurking just beneath the surface of everyday life in many parts of the world. Every now and again, it rises to the surface, signalling a dramatic increase in food insecurity and resulting in famine. **Famine** is defined as a short-term, severe and widespread shortage of food that endangers the lives of the most vulnerable groups and leads to increased mortality (Figure 1.12, page 15).

It is important to understand two concepts that underlie both food insecurity and famine. **Food availability deficit** (FAD) refers to a situation in which there is simply not enough food available to feed a given population. This is clearly the case in virtually all famines. On the other hand, **food entitlement deficit** (FED) occurs when significant numbers of people are unable to pay for the food they need, despite there being food generally available. It is this that can create 'pockets' of food insecurity in an otherwise food-secure country. Such 'pockets' most often coincide with areas of chronic poverty. In the early stages of a famine, it is likely that there will be FED. The initial impact of any growing food shortage will be to push up the price of what little food remains available. Again, it will be the poorest people who suffer FED first.

Famine occurs most frequently in parts of the world that are made particularly vulnerable by contextual factors such as:
- widespread poverty
- a high dependence on farming as a source of income
- poor and inappropriate agricultural practices
- harsh or varying environmental conditions

These factors more or less guarantee a level of food insecurity that is persistently close to the brink of famine. They are essentially endemic, long-term factors. But most famines are short-term and usually triggered by localised 'shocks'. Those shocks can be both 'external', such as wars and migrations, and 'internal', such as a natural disaster or civil war. The disruption of food production quickly leads to FAD.

So the main causes of famine are basically the same as those underlying food insecurity (see Figure 2.5, page 27), but the actual trigger is often provided by a sudden convergence and interplay of localised forces associated with those causes. Most famines are geographically localised and may affect only particular groups within a population, most obviously the poor. The impacts of famine are made worse where there is no safety net in the form of food aid to help the most vulnerable people. These are usually women, children, old people and ethnic minorities. In short, people who have little or no political influence.

Famine is nothing new in the history of humanity. It occurred in the world long before the global population exploded to its present size. Today famine is usually associated with parts of the developing world. In the British Isles, famines occurred until as late as the mid-nineteenth century.

Visit: **www.dfid.gov.uk**

# The causes of famine

It is a popular belief that famines are the outcome of natural events. In 2005 Niger was particularly unlucky to suffer two natural hazards at the same time. But the country's tale of woe did not end there, as its food supply was cut by another famine-inducing event — but one of human origin.

## FAMINE IN NIGER (2005)

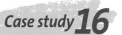
*Case study* **16**

### Triple trouble

Late in the main 2004 rainy season, locusts invaded the scattered crop-growing and livestock-grazing areas of arid northern Niger, causing substantial, but localised, damage to grasslands and crops (Figure 3.1). Shortly afterwards, the rains came to an abrupt halt in many of those areas. This was before the millet and sorghum crops had finished filling their grains, so there was considerable loss of yield (estimated at twice the losses caused by the locusts). Early warnings were given, generally suggesting the likelihood of severe local food insecurity and a need for food aid.

At the same time, another crisis occurred in the south of the country, in what is reckoned to be the relatively wealthy and well watered part of Niger. It is the country's breadbasket. It is also among the more densely populated parts of Africa. Indeed, it is over-populated. Agricultural plots are relatively small and becoming smaller because of population pressure. The pressure on land and the presence of the huge neighbouring Nigerian market are strong incentives to grow commercial crops for export rather than for home consumption.

**Figure 3.1**
*Locust damage —*
*a biological hazard*

Rick Carlson/Fotolia

However, many of the poorer farmers cannot compete in this commercial arena, and have had to sell their land and become wage labourers on cash-crop farms. Both farm owners and labourers often have to supplement the cash they receive, mostly at harvest-time, with loans of grain to support food consumption, but there are long periods when cash and food are in short supply in the household. What tipped the situation in 2005 towards famine was the skyrocketing of basic food prices in tune with global trends.

Niger's 2005 emergency was an amalgam of two different food crises (one due to natural events, the other due to overpopulation) occurring in the same poor country, at the same time, in different locations.

*Famine-initiating droughts and locust plagues are nothing new in this part of Africa. What is new is the deepening degree of underlying poverty and overpopulation and the 'erosion' of subsistence agriculture by the commercial market.*

Even in those cases where natural events such as floods and droughts are regarded as causal factors, it usually requires other factors to convert those events into famines. This is well illustrated by what happened when Cyclone Nargis hit the southern part of Myanmar in May 2008. The famine that followed was largely the result of a government failing to provide the necessary emergency assistance and to accept international food aid.

*Case study* **17** — 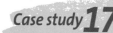 ## DOUBLE TROUBLE IN MYANMAR

### Natural disasters and famine

In May 2008 Cyclone Nargis devastated much of the southern part of Myanmar, causing 4000 deaths, displacing nearly 100 000 people (Figure 3.2) and disrupting food supplies so badly as to create a real risk of famine. The situation was not helped by the apparent inability of the military government to provide the required emergency aid or to accept help from other countries. Four months later, parts of Myanmar were struck by another and rather different natural disaster — a plague of rats.

***Figure 3.2***
*Makeshift shelter in southern Myanmar after Cyclone Nargis struck in May 2008*

Mark Pearson/Alamy

Once every 50 years or so, bamboo plants in the western part of the country produce a fruit. The fruit attracts hordes of rats, which feed on its seeds. These seeds are rich in nutrients and allow the rats to multiply rapidly. Once the seeds have been devoured, the hungry rats turn on villagers' crops, destroying rice and maize and bringing the inhabitants to the brink of starvation.

The Chin region was the part of Myanmar worst hit by the plague of rats. An estimated 20% of the population were thought to be in immediate need of food aid. Since the military government took power in 1962, the Chin people (an ethnic minority) have suffered violent oppression at the hands of the army. Despite appeals, little or no emergency food aid was sent to the area. In desperation, many people migrated and sought food and help in nearby India. Thus it appeared that the Myanmar government took advantage of this natural disaster and its ensuing famine to pursue a policy of ethnic cleansing.

*This case study illustrates the fact that natural disasters are not just geological or climatic. More importantly, it demonstrates that natural disasters can easily be turned into famines when governments fail to provide the necessary emergency aid. Such failure may be because of incompetence or a lack of resources. Equally, it may be that a government, which in this case was an unelected one, takes the opportunity to pursue a rather different agenda, e.g. the persecution of dissident minorities. To decline international offers of aid can be to deprive citizens of their human rights.*

The Myanmar case study also illustrates that famine can be used to pursue other and rather more sinister objectives — in this instance, genocide. The case of the 1932–33 famine in Ukraine is perhaps even more horrifying in that it was deliberately created.

## FAMINE IN THE UKRAINE (1932–33)

*Case study* **18**

### A deliberate act of genocide

In 1917 the Bolshevik Revolution brought to an end tsarist rule in Russia and its colonial territories. One of these territories, the Ukraine, saw this as an opportunity to break away and become an independent republic. This unilateral declaration was strongly resisted by Lenin, principally because the Ukraine was an important food-producing area. Indeed, it was referred to as the 'breadbasket of Europe'. For 4 years, Ukraine sought to protect its territorial integrity. Its army fought Lenin's Red Army and the White Army that had remained loyal to the deposed tsarist regime, as well as invading troops from Poland and other countries. In 1921 the Ukrainian forces were finally defeated. The western part of the Ukraine was divided up between Poland, Romania and Czechoslovakia. The Soviets immediately began shipping out huge amounts of grain to feed the hungry people of Moscow and other big Russian cities. Coincidentally, a drought occurred in the Ukraine, resulting in widespread starvation and a surge of popular resentment against Lenin and the Soviets.

Lenin died in 1924 and was succeeded by Stalin, a ruthless man and even more determined that the Ukraine should remain part of the Soviet Union. Stalin set about a series of actions designed to eliminate any form of Ukrainian independence movement. These included:

- arresting over 5000 Ukrainian scholars who were either shot without trial or deported to prison camps in remote parts of Russia

- imposing the Soviet system of farming known as collectivisation (*Case study 5*) and seizing all privately owned farmland and livestock
- liquidating a class of formerly wealthy farmers called 'kulaks'

But the resistance continued. The Ukrainians simply refused to be cogs in the Soviet farm machine. Wheat and oats were left to rot in unharvested fields as a form of protest.

Stalin responded to the Ukrainian defiance by dictating a policy that would deliberately cause mass starvation. By mid 1932, nearly 75% of the farms in the Ukraine had been forcibly collectivised. On Stalin's orders, mandatory quotas of foodstuffs to be shipped from the Ukraine to other parts of the Soviet Union were drastically increased in August, October and again in January 1933, until there was simply no food remaining to feed the people of the Ukraine.

Much of the abundant wheat crop harvested by the Ukrainians in 1933 was dumped on the foreign market to generate cash to aid Stalin's plan for the modernisation of the Soviet Union and also to help finance his massive military build-up. It is estimated that if the wheat had remained in the Ukraine, it would have been enough to feed all the people there for up to 2 years.

Starvation quickly followed throughout the Ukraine, with the most vulnerable, children and the elderly, being the first to feel the effects of malnutrition. In desperation, hordes of people abandoned the countryside and set off in search of food in the towns and cities. But there was none to be had. It has been estimated that Stalin's artificially induced famine killed more than 7 million people in the Ukraine — one of the last places on Earth where a famine might have been expected.

*This is probably the most blatant example in modern history of a famine being contrived to achieve a geopolitical objective.*

Famines are not always the result of food shortages brought on by some sort of catastrophic natural event. They can occur where there is a breakdown in the marketing system that links food production with food consumption or when governments put other national considerations above the welfare of their people.

## Case study 19  FAMINE IN NORTH KOREA

### Why so?

North Korea, a small, backward and isolated country with a centralised economy, was hit by a prolonged famine during the mid-1990s. As with most famines, the trigger was a natural hazard in the form of unprecedented floods. But what really converted an emergency into a famine was the collapse of the Soviet Union, which for decades had supplied food to North Korea at 'friendship prices'. Moreover, the break-up of the Soviet Union dealt a double blow. Not only did North Korea lose its source of cheap food, it also lost the main market for its economic output in the form of industrial and agricultural products. Inevitably the economy spiralled into decline and the government was powerless to do much to stave off the threatened famine.

One indication of the desperateness of the situation was the government propaganda extolling the virtues of having two meals a day instead of three. Later food rationing coupons were issued, but by now the distribution of food was breaking down and, as a result, the shops were empty. It was with reluctance that the North Korean government accepted food aid from the USA and China. The aid was gradually withdrawn, however, when it was discovered being diverted to feed the military and being sold on the open market. Nearly 1 million people starved to death.

Over the last decade or so, the North Korean government has become increasingly reclusive and unpredictable. It also suffers from delusions of military grandeur, seemingly intent upon becoming a nuclear power and maintaining a military force that is truly oversized for such a small country. The 'pantomime' parades that periodically appear on our television screens are meant to impress the outside world with its military might. Equally, they can be seen as evidence of a government that misuses its resources and callously puts the basic welfare of its people well down its list of priorities.

In 2008 North Korea was again on the brink of famine. The gap between the required amount of grain and available supply was around 100 000 metric tonnes. Local food prices more than trebled. International food aid was again reluctantly accepted, but with its distribution being much more closely monitored by its donors. The aid may have just about kept the famine at arm's length. The daily food rations for North Koreans on the public distribution system now stand at 350 calories. In contrast, the average daily food intake in the USA is over 3000 calories.

There is a strong likelihood that North Korea will continue to be confronted by chronic food security problems and periodic famines unless some long-term corrective steps are taken. Most important is the need to revitalise its manufacturing and to move out of its isolation and into the trading world. The export of industrial products would earn foreign currency that could be used to import grains and other foodstuffs to make good the shortfalls in domestic food production. In the interim, it should enter into negotiations with the World Food Programme, accept more food aid and guarantee its proper distribution.

The key questions here are:
- Is it possible to make the country's centralised economy more efficient and productive?
- Is North Korea ready or willing to normalise its relations with the global community?
- Will the welfare of its people ever become a priority?

*North Korea has been described as belonging to the 'axis of evil', a term used by President George W. Bush to describe states guilty of helping terrorism and seeking weapons of mass destruction. Ironically, it seems that North Korea's autocratic regime also stands guilty of attempting the mass destruction of its own people — by malnutrition and famine.*

## 16 | Question

**Using case studies**

**Distinguish between 'food insecurity' and 'famine'.**

### Guidance

Identify the differences between the two terms with regard to (a) their symptoms, and (b) their causes. Be sure to make use of the case studies in this and the previous parts of the book to illustrate the points you wish to make.

### Question

**'Not all famines are caused by environmental hazards.' To what extent do you agree with this statement? Use case studies to support your argument.**

### Guidance

Most famines have multiple causes, and in nearly all these cases there is an environmental factor. It often just needs an event such as a war, civil unrest or government indifference to trigger the onset of famine. There are plenty of examples of famines to support the statement (e.g. Darfur — *Case study 13*). There are some famines that can be laid at the door of natural hazards (e.g. Niger and Ireland — *Case studies 16 and 22*). The Ukrainian and North Korean famines (*Case studies 18 and 19*) can be cited in support of the statement.

What emerges from these case studies is that governments have a particular responsibility to alert the outside world and seek aid before famine strikes. Famines rarely happen overnight. They can be spotted looming on the horizon. Furthermore, in most cases there is a 'window of opportunity' between the occurrence of a natural disaster and the onset of any consequent famine. It is worrying to recall how many governments have failed to do anything during this window. It is even more worrying to know that governments have used famine to further other sinister objectives.

# Famine relief

Most famine situations eventually receive emergency food aid, most if not all of it coming from outside the afflicted country. Such international aid comes through three different donor routes:

- **bilateral aid** — provided directly by one country, such as by China to North Korea
- **multilateral aid** — provided by a number of countries through the medium of a third-party intergovernmental organisation, of which by far the biggest is the UN World Food Programme
- **non-governmental aid** — provided through any number of voluntary organisations, such as the Red Cross and Oxfam

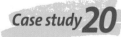

*Case study 20*   THE UN WORLD FOOD PROGRAMME

### Relieving famines

The World Food Programme (WFP) is the branch of the United Nations responsible for food aid. It is claimed to be the world's largest humanitarian organisation. On average, it provides food (4 million metric tonnes) to 90 million people per year, two-thirds of whom are children (Figure 3.3). Its headquarters are in Rome and it runs 80 country offices around the world. It was set up in 1960.

The basic aim of the WFP is to eradicate hunger and malnutrition, with the ultimate goal being to eliminate the need for food aid itself. The WFP's brief is much broader than just the relief of famines and other emergency situations. Food aid is also directed to fight micronutrient deficiencies, reduce child mortality, improve maternal health,

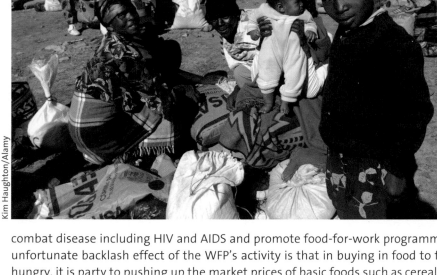

*Figure 3.3*
*A WFP aid distribution point in Lesotho provides food for people affected by poverty*

Kim Haughton/Alamy

combat disease including HIV and AIDS and promote food-for-work programmes. One unfortunate backlash effect of the WFP's activity is that in buying in food to feed the hungry, it is party to pushing up the market prices of basic foods such as cereals.

**18**

**Using case studies**

Visit the World Food Programme website www.wfp.org and find out what the organisation has been doing in one of the case study countries in this and previous parts of the book, for example Ethiopia, Sudan, Zimbabwe, Niger, Myanmar or North Korea.

**Guidance**

Are you able to distinguish between what the WFP has done by way of a short-term emergency response to the threat of famine and by longer-term help to reduce malnutrition and food insecurity?

# Life on the margins

It is worth clarifying what is meant by the 'margins' in this context of food and famine. There are two possible and slightly different connotations. One refers to the spatial limits of where it is possible to grow food (the so-called margin of cultivation). These are largely determined by physical conditions (low temperatures, aridity and infertile soils) and economic factors (commodity prices and demand). The second refers to the margin that critically separates food security from food insecurity, feasting from famine, and survival from starvation. It is this margin that is now brought into focus.

If nothing else, it is hoped that the case studies in this part of the book have rammed home one critical point, namely the significance of poverty. It is the poor who are most vulnerable to food insecurity and famines. Being poor is generally viewed in terms of deprivation of some of life's basic needs, such as food, clean water, housing, clothing, basic education, primary healthcare and security. Why are the poor so vulnerable to hunger and starvation? There are a number of interrelated explanations that together create a sort of downward spiral:

- Poor families are either landless or have access only to the most marginal of farmland, which is likely to be the first to feel the impact of any natural disaster.
- Food shortages raise the price of food, which the poor cannot afford.
- There is a high prevalence of ill-health among the poor for a variety of reasons — no access to primary healthcare, unsafe water supply and sewage disposal. A poor diet weakens resistance to a wide range of diseases (*Case study 21*).
- The poor have little or no political 'voice' with which to publicise their plight or to fight for food.

As a consequence, mortality rates among the poor and particularly their children are all too readily raised even by the slightest increase in food insecurity, let alone a famine.

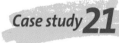

*Case study* 21 — DISEASES OF FAMINE

### Critical nutrient deficiencies

*Table 3.1
Nutrient-deficiency
diseases*

It is only during prolonged famines that the lack of food becomes a direct cause of death. The rise in the mortality rate is due more to people falling victim to diseases related to undernutrition and malnutrition. The causal factors are deficiencies in the intake of certain vital nutrients (Table 3.1).

| Nutrient | Function | Source | Deficiency disease | Symptoms | Scale of disease |
|---|---|---|---|---|---|
| Vitamin A | Vision; body growth and healing | Milk, cheese, liver and fish | Xerophthalmia | Poor sight, blindness, reduced resistance to infection | Affects 50% of children in the developing world |
| Vitamin B | Release of energy | Liver, some grains and pulses | Pellagra | Weight loss, diarrhoea, mental disorder | Prevalent where maize diets predominate |
| Vitamin B1 | Release of energy; nerves | Grains, milk, eggs, dried peas and beans | Beriberi | Loss of appetite, swelling, heart failure | Prevalent where overcooking predominates |
| Vitamin C | Wound healing, iron absorption | Citrus and other fruits; potatoes and green vegetables | Scurvy | Slow healing of wounds; bone weakening | Not known |
| Vitamin D | Calcium absorption | Sunlight, dairy produce, oily fish | Rickets and osteomalacia | Bone deformities | Prevalent where insufficient exposure to sunlight |
| Protein | Growth and repair of body tissues | Meat, cheese, eggs, nuts and pulses | Malnutrition — kwashiorkor and osteomalacia | Muscle wasting and weight loss | Affects about a quarter of the population of the developing world |
| Iron | Formation of red blood cells | Liver, meat, vegetables with green leaves | Anaemia | Blood disorders causing fatigue, loss of appetite and low blood pressure | Affects 917 million people, especially women in the developing world |
| Iodine | Vital to brain activity | Fish, seafood, eggs, milk and cheese | Stillbirths, endemic cretinism, goitre | Brain damage and mental retardation | 600 million people affected |

*Contemporary Case Studies*

During times of food shortage and famine it is infants and children who suffer most — their mortality rates are raised much more than those of adults. Why? One factor is that maternal malnutrition during pregnancy means that a baby's resistance to deficiency diseases is already weakened. Infants are also vulnerable to diseases related to other conditions that frequently accompany a famine, such as unclean water, poor sewage disposal and inadequate access to primary healthcare.

*There is a wide range of diseases associated in general with famine and in particular with specific nutrient deficiencies.*

A common reaction to food shortages and famines is migration. People are simply persuaded that the only option open to them in their desperate search for food is to seek it somewhere else. Again, it is the poor who figure most prominently in such population movements. The classic case study in this context is the Irish potato famine of 1845–50 and its outward ripples of migration (*Case study 22*). Today, the mass media regularly transmit grim images of emaciated and weary people carrying their children and a few possessions in a desperate search for food (*Case study 23*). For these people, the term '**food miles**' has a particular meaning — long and sometimes fruitless journeys on foot.

## IRELAND'S GREAT HUNGER

Case study 22

### Depart or die

The potato famine that hit Ireland between 1845 and 1850 killed 1 million people (nearly one-eighth of the total population). The famine was caused by a fungal disease or blight that devastated the potato harvest, the potato being the country's staple

*Figure 3.4*
*Famine memorial sculptures on Custom House Quay, Dublin — many emigrants departed from this quay for Liverpool and other parts of the world*

food. The situation was not helped by a high dependence on this single crop, by the considerable growth in the Irish population and by the fact that Ireland continued to export food to England during the crisis. Added to all this, the British government was misguided in the type of help it provided — launching public works projects rather than trying to diversify and increase food production.

Many people faced with starvation and the likelihood of premature death decided to emigrate (Figure 3.4).

It is estimated that as many Irish emigrated as died from starvation — 1 million. Prior to the potato famine, it is reckoned that about 5000 Irish immigrants were arriving in the USA each year. That number rose astronomically as the famine gripped. By 1850 the population of New York City was estimated to be one-quarter Irish. Canada also opened its doors to the Irish, as did Britain. Today people of Irish ancestry (much of it dating from potato famine immigration) account for at least 10% of the UK's population. That percentage figure is considerably higher in Liverpool, parts of Lancashire and London. The migration ripples also reached as far as Australia and South America, but with smaller numbers involved.

*Famine in Ireland in the nineteenth century caused by a persistent potato blight helps to explain the present distribution of people of Irish descent in particular parts of the world.*

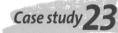 **Case study 23** ENVIRONMENTAL REFUGEES

### An integral part of life on the margins

Environmental refugees are people who can no longer gain a secure livelihood in their homeland because of drought, soil erosion, desertification and other environmental problems. They are the face of the environmental impacts illustrated in Part 3 and of life on the margins.

It is estimated that today there are well over 25 million environmental refugees, or nearly 0.5% of the world's population — one person in every 200. By comparison, a figure of 18 million is given for those who are officially recognised as 'refugees' — people who are forced to move for political, religious or ethnic reasons. Many environmental refugee migrations take place within rather than across national frontiers. For this reason, they do not hit the headlines very often and may be seriously underestimated. Migrations across national frontiers are more newsworthy because of the political tensions they so often cause.

If present trends continue, the number of environmental refugees could well reach 200 million by 2050 (potentially equivalent to 2% of the global population). In short, environmental refugees are fast becoming one of the foremost human crises of our time. The costs are enormous in terms of the trauma, stress and alienation acutely felt by individual migrants.

Given that the main 'push' factors are food insecurity, hunger and famine, the solution to the environmental refugee challenge seems likely to lie in:

■ finding modes of food production that are sustainable in such difficult environments (see Part 6)
■ spreading the necessary know-how
■ putting the brake on population growth and thus easing the overpopulation underlying so much of this migration

Such pre-emptive actions, which tackle the sources of the problem, are a better long-term bet than directing scarce resources to setting up refugee camps and embarking on resettlement programmes that rarely succeed.

*Many of the headline-hitting migrations of recent times have been the reaction to famines induced by environmental hazards and civil strife. But they have also been exacerbated by climate change.*

So life on the margins is very much about poverty, hunger and sometimes starvation. It is also about dependence on international aid and on governments that do not always have the best interests of their people in mind. Life on the margins can also be punctuated by spells of forced migration and refugee status.

**19** **Question**

**With the aid of examples, explain what 'life on the margins' really means.**

**Guidance**

The last paragraph gives you the main features of life on the margins: now explain and illustrate each of them. You might start by researching the following websites:

www.geographyinthenews.rgs.org/news/article/?id=766
www.secularpakistan.wordpress.com/.../pakistans-baloch-life-on-the-margins-of-punjab

# Power players in the global food chain

## The geopolitics of food

Geopolitics is about the structure and distribution of global power. In an era of increasing economic globalisation, food has joined energy and water as geopolitical commodities. This has happened not so much because of any overall scarcity as through the spatial mismatch between food production and food consumption. The **human food chain** from farmer to consumer is increasingly in the hands of a relatively small number of key players who wield their power and influence at an international and even global level.

At the food producing end, the major geopolitical players are national governments and agribusinesses (see Figure 1, page vi). At the consumer end, the major food retailers hold sway. When it comes to the transfer of food from producer to consumer, the key players are international organisations such as the FAO, the World Bank and the WTO. With their interests overarching all or most of the stages in the human food chain are the transnational companies such as Unilever, Monsanto and Nestlé.

## Food production — key players

Government intervention is now recognised as a major influence on agriculture and food production. That intervention can range from a 'gentle touch on the tiller' through systems that steer in a particular direction, to tight control over both the inputs and outputs of farming. There are varying degrees of government intervention in all if not most HICs; New Zealand is a notable exception. There is significantly less intervention, if any, in LICs. The greatest intervention occurs, of course, in the so-called 'planned' economies of the socialist world. Figure 4.1 indicates the main motives for government intervention in food production.

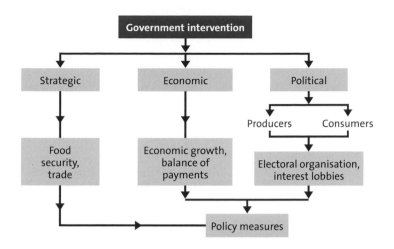

**Figure 4.1**
*Government
intervention*

## THE COMMON AGRICULTURAL POLICY

Case study 24

### Balancing food production and consumption

The European Union (EU) introduced its Common Agricultural Policy (CAP) in 1963, with the following aims:

- to increase agricultural productivity
- to ensure a fair standard of living for the agricultural population of the EU
- to stabilise markets
- to guarantee regular supplies of food products
- to ensure reasonable prices of supplies to consumers

The policy made progress on the first four objectives, but at the expense of the fifth. Consumers have had to pay for the success of the farming sector, not only through higher food prices (almost invariably higher than world prices), but also through taxes to support an EU budget geared to supporting farmers.

A controversial part of the CAP was the system of 'intervention prices' set for a range of agricultural products. This was basically to compensate farmers by means of subsidies if commodity market prices happened to fall. The outcome of this policy was to constantly stimulate overproduction. The surpluses gave rise to journalistic labels such as the 'butter mountain' and the 'wine lake'.

Changes to the CAP were made in 1991 and 2000, not just to reduce the surpluses but also to make EU agriculture more environmentally acceptable. Still more significant reforms were made in 2003. They included:

- 'decoupling' — breaking the link between subsidy and the level of production and so reducing the likelihood of surpluses
- encouraging farmers to produce for the market rather than for the subsidies
- reducing the environmental impacts of farming by removing the incentive for farmers to maximise production
- raising support for rural development and environmental conservation, with farmers paid to be 'stewards' of the countryside
- reducing red tape

The enlargement of the EU in 2004 has raised some new challenges for the CAP. The nub of the problem is that the new member states are more dependent on farming as a source of income and employment. There is an expectation among them that they should receive the same level of support as was provided to the early members of the EU. But times have changed. There is now a better balance between food production and consumption and a better awareness of the environmental risks associated with more intensive modes of farming. The main tension within the EU today is between those states where farms are large and efficient (the Netherlands, Sweden and the UK) and those states where farming is significantly less efficient (France and newcomers such as Poland and Romania). These two camps are at odds with each other over the level of support that should be provided by the CAP.

Finally, it should be noted that the CAP has not been popular at a global level. The EU has been accused by the World Trade Organization of unfairly protecting both its food producers and food markets from outside competition (*Case study 26*).

*Over the years, the CAP has been the target of much criticism and even ridicule. However, in recent decades the package of policy measures has produced some successes within the three arenas of government intervention shown in Figure 4.1. Not least of these has been the overall improvement in EU food security. But the large slice of the EU budget taken each year by the CAP has made them very expensive achievements.*

## 20 Question

**Look at Figure 4.1. How would you classify the interventions made by the CAP in EU food production? Give your reasons.**

### Guidance

Which of the three headings — strategic, economic and political — best applies? Two other questions for you to consider include: might more than one heading apply, and might an additional heading be required?

*Using case studies*

While global agriculture is increasingly influenced by individual governments and by groupings of governments such as the EU and the North American Free Trade Agreement (NAFTA), there are other significant developments at the food-producing end of the food chain. One is the 'industrialisation' of agriculture in many parts of the world, particularly the HICs. This is the product of the third agricultural revolution (*Case study 1*). It represents the latest stage in the evolution of the agricultural curve (see Figure 1.1, page 3).

At the same time, food production is becoming a much more 'capitalised' activity. Money is now being invested in some of its branches on an unprecedented scale. These two processes of industrialisation and capitalisation have found expression in a relative newcomer to food production: corporate farming, otherwise known as **agribusiness.**

*Case study* **25** AGRIBUSINESS

### The what, why and wherefore

The interests of agribusiness, sometimes referred to as corporate farming as distinct from family farming, are wider than just producing food. Its activities extend to other links in the human food chain (Figure 1, page vi). For example, it often includes downstream links to the processing, storing and packaging of food and its delivery to major retailing outlets, as well as upstream links to seed companies and livestock research stations.

Traditionally, big investors have shown little interest in agriculture. But that has now changed. Before and even after the 2007–09 credit crunch, banks have become keen to lend money to the farming industry, especially agribusiness. The underlying reason has been the boom in food retailing and the ever-rising public demand for cheap and exotic foods. The particular appeal of an agribusiness as a target for investment lies in the fact that it involves:

- creating food production chains that are controlled by a single company
- specialising in particular food products
- capitalising on scale economies

In Europe, it is somewhat ironic that not all agribusinesses own farms, but rather they own businesses 'upstream' and 'downstream' of the farm, particularly the latter. Such firms enter into renewable contracts with farmers. Farmers agree to sell to the agribusiness their output of specified products at fixed prices. This is known as forward contracting. The price is agreed before cultivation or rearing begins. Such contracts are to the advantage of the agribusiness, as the risks of production (unfavourable weather, disease etc.) are borne by the farmer. Not owning the farm also allows the agribusiness more flexibility to 'shop around' for the best (i.e. the lowest) commodity prices.

The shape of agriculture and the future of rural society in virtually all HICs now lie in the hands of agribusiness together with the supermarkets and the food-oriented **transnational corporations** (TNCs) (*Case study 29*). The growth of agribusiness has been to the detriment of the family farm. Those that contract to agribusinesses lose their independence. Other family farms have been driven to amalgamate into larger holdings in order to remain competitive. They have also been encouraged to increase their specialisation.

*The agribusiness is a new arrival in the human food chain, but its sheer scale and diverse activities now make it an important player in terms of what foods are produced and in what quantities.*

More recently, agribusiness has spread to the LICs, as customers in HIC supermarkets look for exotic and 'out-of-season' fruits and vegetables that can be grown in the tropics and sub-tropics virtually throughout the year. This southward spread of agribusiness has been largely through the efforts of the food-oriented TNCs (*Case study 29*). Here the impact of corporate agriculture threatens to be even more profound, especially on subsistence farmers (*Case study 3*).

**21** **Using case studies**

### Question
**Explain the advantages to an agribusiness of being involved in more than one link in the human food chain.**

### Guidance
Explore and explain the following ideas — risk-spreading and reduced vulnerability to pressures from other businesses in the chain.

# Food transfers — key players

The global transfers of food from producers to consumers provide a geopolitical arena that has encouraged the emergence of powerful and influential organisations operating at a global level. The next case study looks at just two rather different organisations — one driven by humanitarian concerns and the other by the need to avoid trade wars over food, and indeed other commodities. Both in their own way seek to achieve a more food-secure world.

*Case study 26* THE FAO AND THE WTO

## Two different global players

The Food and Agriculture Organization (FAO) of the United Nations was set up in 1945. It leads international efforts to defeat hunger and improve food security, largely in conjunction with its sister agency the World Food Programme (*Case study 20*). That is the principal objective, but it also has a number of subsidiary functions:

- The FAO serves both developing and developed countries by providing a neutral forum in which all nations can debate global policy and negotiate agreements.
- It is a source of knowledge. It collects information from all over the world that can help countries, especially developing ones, to modernise not only their agriculture but also their forestry and fisheries.
- It disseminates information about good nutrition and diets.
- It helps member countries to devise and implement agricultural policies aimed at alleviating hunger and achieving rural development.

In short, the FAO has considerable clout at an international level based on over 60 years of experience. In food-related issues it is widely respected throughout the global community.

The World Trade Organization (WTO) started life in 1947 when it was known as the General Agreement on Tariffs and Trade (GATT). It was set up after the Second World War in order to promote free trade by removing tariffs and other types of trade barrier. In 1995 it was renamed the WTO. It is the only global organisation dealing with the rules of trade between nations. Its headquarters are in Geneva (Switzerland), and 153 of the world's countries are now members.

Given the mismatch between the global patterns of food production and food consumption, food is a major commodity in today's world trade. For this reason alone, the potential influence of the WTO is immense.

It has to be said that the achievements of the WTO are modest and that it has been the subject of negative publicity. Some people see it as an organisation that is looking after the best interests of the HICs rather than those of the LICs. They claim that the global trade 'playing field' remains distinctly uneven (i.e. unfair). The WTO has done little to reduce trade friction, for example that between the EU and the USA over agricultural subsidies. A basic weakness of the organisation is that each member state reserves the right to protect its own trading interests when it believes those interests are being adversely affected. Exercise of that right is hardly likely to produce a truly free trade in food or indeed in any other commodity.

Visit: **www.fao.org** and **www.wto.org**

*The FAO and the WTO are rather different major players — one is focused on food production and the other is concerned with bridging the spatial gap between food producers and consumers. As yet, the achievements of the former outshine those of the latter.*

**Using case studies**

**22**

**Research the reasons why the WTO has achieved little in terms of liberalising the international trade in food.**

**Guidance**

Investigate the relationships between three international groupings: the EU and Japan; the USA and the Cairns Group; and the LICs. You might focus on a controversial commodity such as sugar.

# Food consumption — key players

Power players have become very evident in the human food chain, particularly at the production and processing stages (Figure 1, page vi).

The distribution and retailing of food today is big business, and it is no surprise that big businesses have moved into this market in a big way. The players are household names: Wal-Mart, Carrefour, Tesco and Sainsbury's — the supermarket chains.

## THE RISE AND SPREAD OF TESCO

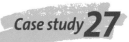
*Case study 27*

### A remarkable record

Tesco was founded in 1924. The name of the company was based on those of the man who set it up, Jack Cohen, and his first supplier, T.E. Stockwell. At first, it simply sold groceries in London's East End markets. Its first store was opened in 1929 in Edgware (northwest London).

In more than 80 years of operation, the company has come a remarkably long way. It has become Britain's leading food retailer, with branches in all parts of the UK. In recent years it has successfully sought to broaden its business in a number of ways:

- It has diversified its typical locations in the UK with its mix of out-of-town/edge-of-town superstores and its branches of Tesco Express, Tesco Extra and Tesco Metro in suburban and inner urban locations (Figure 4.2). There are few areas in the British Isles that are beyond convenient reach of a branch of Tesco.
- It has extended its business overseas, first to Ireland and mainland Europe, then to Asia and most recently to the USA.
- It has diversified its business in the UK into non-food retailing — clothing, electrical and electronic goods, furniture and household goods. One of Tesco's five objectives is to be as strong in non-food as in food retailing.
- It is now diversifying beyond retailing into services — financial, insurance, telecoms, tesco.com etc.

Tesco

**Figure 4.2**
**Four types of Tesco store**

Today, Tesco is the largest UK retailer in terms of both its global sales and its domestic market share, with annual profits exceeding £3 billion. It is currently the third-largest global retailer in terms of revenue, behind the USA's Wal-Mart and France's Carrefour, but is ranked second in terms of profits, ahead of Carrefour. Tesco's market share in the UK is just over 30%.

*There is no doubt that the emergence of large supermarket chains has done much to change our lifestyles, from where and how we shop for food to how much and what we eat.*

The rise and spread of Tesco and other supermarket chains both here and in other parts of the world has changed the face of food retailing in the developed world. They have changed where we shop, how we shop, when we shop and what we buy and consume. They are also responsible for the way food is packaged and for that vital 'ingredient' in the diet of everyday life in HICs — convenience food. They have undoubtedly brought benefits to their growing ranks of customers in the form of relatively cheap food. Keen competition between chains has helped. Also, their size means that some of the economies achieved by the scale of super-market purchasing and operating can be passed on to the customer. But at the same time their growth has brought about the closure of many small shops and has contributed to the 'cloning' of the High Street and other retailing areas. There is also growing concern that so much of food retailing in large parts of the world is in the hands of a small number of companies. Might we be fast approaching a monopoly situation that ultimately allows these giants to hold their customers to ransom? Finally, it seems likely that the large supermarket chains stand guilty of

*Contemporary Case Studies*

increasing food insecurity in parts of the developing world by encouraging **land grabbing** (*Case study 48*) and the conversion of subsistence into commercial farmland (*Case study 3*). Does retaining the loyalty of the British shopper really hang on providing exotic and 'out-of-season' fruit and vegetables grown on land formerly given over to subsistence farming? Think too about the environmental costs of the food miles involved (*Case study 34*).

It needs to be remembered that the supermarkets and the neighbourhood '24–7' shops are not the only ways in which food finally reaches the customers in the developed world. There is a diversity of outlets serving prepared food, from the hotel to the fish-and-chip shop, from the four-star restaurant to the cosy 'olde worlde' tearoom, from the motorway service area to the vending machine.

This whole field of catering and our modern lifestyles have created huge business opportunities that have been exploited by powerful companies. Perhaps the most obvious of these are the fast food outlets, both eat-in and take-away. The big players here are also household names — McDonald's, KFC, Burger King, Pizza Hut, Starbucks etc.

## FAST FOOD

*Case study* **28**

### The story of the Big Mac
McDonald's opened its first outlet in the UK in 1974. Today, more than 2.5 million people in the UK patronise a branch of McDonald's every day. Customers trust it to provide them with food of a safe standard, quick service and value for money. There are currently more than 1000 McDonald's outlets throughout the UK. They range in location from the high street to the motorway drive-in.

**Figure 4.3**
*Global spread of McDonald's since 1940*

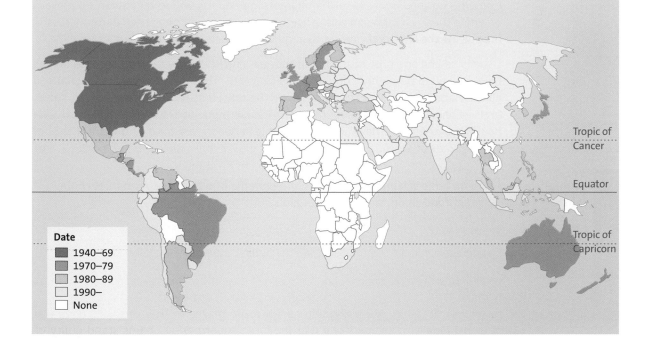

Legend:
Date
- 1940–69
- 1970–79
- 1980–89
- 1990–
- None

Tropic of Cancer

Equator

Tropic of Capricorn

McDonald's is the third-largest (after Yum! and Subway) but best-known fast-food provider, with more than 31000 outlets in 120 countries (Figures 4.3 and 4.4). It is reckoned to serve food to 47 million customers each day and directly employ 1.5 million people. Behind McDonald's and the other fast-food giants is a vast food-processing industry, duty-bound to produce, at knock-down prices, a consistent product that satisfies the food safety standards of the outlet country. Behind the burger-maker is a livestock-rearing network that spans much of the world and 'consumes' the output of much arable land.

**Figure 4.4**
*McDonald's in Shanghai*

A critical part of its global spread has been to take into account local eating traditions. It is no good trying to sell hamburgers in a country where vegetarianism prevails or where there is a taboo on eating beef or pork. McDonald's has been quite successful in applying the fast-food concept to non-Western diets (Figure 4.4).

Usually selling one type of meal (hamburger, chicken or pizza), the fast-food chains have proved to be highly popular and successful. They have undoubtedly changed eating habits, but not necessarily for the better. First, they tempt us to eat more, and second, there is little room for a regular input of traditional fast food in a healthy diet. Studies have indicated a link between fast food and rising levels of obesity (*Case study 8*).

**23** Compile a two-column table setting out the costs and benefits of either a supermarket chain, such as Tesco, or a fast-food chain, such as McDonald's.

*Using case studies*

**Guidance**

Try to set aside any preconceptions or prejudices you might have either for or against such companies.

# Transnational corporations

The distinction between agribusiness and TNCs needs to be clarified. Some TNCs, but only a minority, are involved in agribusiness, while there are many agribusinesses that have no links at all with TNCs. Significant differences include the following:

■ TNCs are much bigger businesses and operate almost exclusively on an international scale.

■ TNCs are active in economic fields that have nothing to do with agriculture, notably manufacturing and services.

■ Those TNCs with a particular interest in food are most active in the processing and distribution stages of the human food chain. The names of such companies are well known, and include Nestlé, Unilever, Kraft, General Foods, Coca Cola, Rank Hovis McDougall and Nabisco. Agribusinesses are focused on production (Figure 1, page vi).

Both TNCs and agribusinesses are in their different ways contributing to the globalisation of agriculture and food supply. Visit the following website: **www.agribusiness accountability.org**

## NESTLÉ AND UNILEVER
Case study 29

### Food giants

The Swiss giant Nestlé was founded in 1866 and ranks second only to Unilever in the global league table of TNCs involved in the food and beverage industry. Over 90% of its sales revenue comes from food and drink, with nearly half its sales in Europe, a quarter in North America and about 10% in Latin America and Asia. It employs about a quarter of a million people worldwide and operates nearly 500 factories in 70 countries.

Unilever, an Anglo-Dutch company incorporated in 1927, is a supplier of consumer goods in the food, household care and personal product categories. It embraces some 500 brand name companies in more than 80 countries and employs in the order of 300 000 people worldwide. It is the global leader so far as processed food products are concerned. This sector accounts for just over half its total business. It also has other operations, the most significant being its plantations growing palm oil, tea, coconuts and rubber.

*Table 4.1
Some brand names in the Nestlé and Unilever portfolios*

| Food category | Some Nestlé brand names | Some Unilever brand names |
|---|---|---|
| Beverages | Milo, Nescafé, Nesquik, Vittel, Perrier | Brooke Bond, Lipton, Lyons, PG Tips |
| Milk products (including ice cream) | Carnation, Chambourcy, Coffee-mate, Lyons Maid | Ben & Jerry's, Magnum, Wall's, Solero, Cornetto, Carte d'Or, Viennetta |
| Margarines, spreads, oils and cooking fats | | Flora, Stork, Bertolli, Puget, Rama, Becel |
| Chocolate and confectionery | Kit Kat, Polo, Milky Bar | |
| Prepared dishes and cooking aids | Bavarois, Buitoni, Chambourcy, Crosse & Blackwell, Findus, Libby's, Maggi, Stouffer's | Bovril, Knorr, Marmite, Coleman's, Pot Noodle |

*Table 4.1 gives a flavour of the involvement of these two TNCs in the food sector alone. It shows that both have been highly acquisitive in taking over famous brand names. Their fields of operation (both processing and distribution) are truly global.*

**24**

*Using case studies*

## Question

**Explain and illustrate the difference between an agribusiness and a TNC with particular interests in the food business.**

### Guidance

You will need to re-read *Case Studies 25 and 29*. Possible criteria for structuring the comparison include size, spatial scale of operation, range of interests, and organisation.

**25**

*Using case studies*

**Research the TNC Monsanto (www.monsanto.com) and compare it with either Nestlé or Unilever.**

### Guidance

Focus on the particular interests of both TNCs. To what extent do they compete with or complement each other?

Finally, having looked at a small selection of the different power players in the global food chain, perhaps you share the view that both (a) the balance of power and (b) the benefits of the globalisation of food production and supply brought about by these players tip in favour of the developed world.

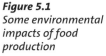

# The environmental impacts of food production

It would be true to say that virtually all types of food production mark and change the natural environment in one way or another. Indeed, food production generally has created its own distinctive landscapes. This is hardly surprising, bearing in mind that food production is the world's largest single user of land and one of the oldest economic activities. Figure 5.1 shows some of the environmental impacts of food production. Each of the five main headings will be illustrated by a single case study.

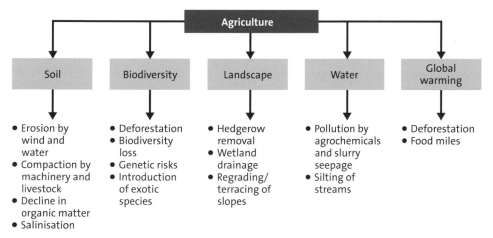

*Figure 5.1*
*Some environmental impacts of food production*

## Soil

To many people, the most obvious consequence of farming is soil erosion. This occurs when the surface layer of productive topsoil is removed by either wind or water. While it is a 'natural' process encouraged by particular combinations of climate, relief, soil and vegetation, there is no doubt that in many instances it is made far worse by people. This is particularly so when the natural vegetation cover is removed as a prelude to farming. It is also exacerbated at times when the soil is exposed, as between crops or when pasture has been overgrazed. Soil lost to wind and water ranges from 5–10 tonnes per hectare annually in Africa, Europe and Australia to 10–20 tonnes in the Americas and nearly 30 tonnes in Asia.

There is no doubt about the seriousness of soil erosion in terms of rendering food-growing land useless. But coming an unhealthy second is **salinisation** (*Case study 30*).

## Case study 30 — SALINISATION IN BANGLADESH

### The downside to irrigation
In many parts of the world, especially the drier ones, irrigation is used to help raise crop yields and improve livestock grazing. The achievements have been considerable, but there is a growing realisation that irrigation also has its risks in terms of the environment. Such risks are well illustrated in Bangladesh. They include:

- pumping water from rivers and wells at an unsustainable rate. This lowers the water table and requires wells to be sunk to greater depths. In the case of Bangladesh, shallow tube wells are becoming waterless.
- the contamination of Bangladesh's groundwater by arsenic, which occurs naturally in some of the rocks. Using this water on crops means that the poison can enter the human food chain.
- excessive irrigation, leading to the ground becoming waterlogged. This is not good for plant life.

But the risk that has materialised into a serious hazard in Bangladesh is salinisation. There are two types of salinisation; both are linked to irrigation. First, water that has been used to irrigate the soil evaporates during the dry season that follows the heavy monsoon rains. This causes salts to form a pan within the upper layers of the soil. The salt pan is poisonous to crops and lethal to plant life. Second, salinisation results from the excessive withdrawal of underground water in coastal areas not just for irrigation but also for industry and human consumption. This leads to the intrusion of marine (saline) water into freshwater arteries and the groundwater.

*Figure 5.2*
*Process of salinisation in irrigated areas in the tropics*

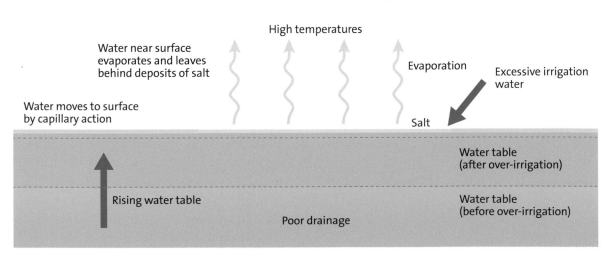

The salinisation of Bangladesh's water has destroyed rice farming in many areas, where it has been replaced by the less labour-intensive prawn farming. The outcome is basically a loss of subsistence food and employment but a gain in commercial food that finds its way into the country's exports. It has thus not helped reduce the level of food insecurity in Bangladesh.

The prospects for Bangladesh in the era of global warming are especially grim. Not only will large areas of farmland be inundated, but that which remains will be made sterile by increasing salinisation.

*Many think that irrigation is vital to increased food production, but it does have a serious downside in the form of salinisation. Over-pumping of groundwater in coastal areas is also a cause of salinisation.*

## 26 Question

**Why is salinisation expected to increase with global warming?**

### Guidance

Drier climates are likely to increase desertification and the need for irrigation. Rising sea levels are likely to increase salinisation in new coastal areas.

# Biodiversity

The clearance of forest to create agricultural land not only aggravates soil erosion but also has an adverse environmental impact in its own right, often leading to degradation and a serious loss of biodiversity as well as contributing to global warming. Nearly 17 million hectares of tropical forest disappear each year as a result of deforestation — that is, about 1% of the total.

## DEFORESTATION IN BRAZIL

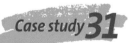
*Case study 31*

### For food, fuel and a future of biodiversity loss

Between 2000 and 2007, Brazil lost around 150 000 km$^2$ of forest — an area larger than Greece — and since 1970 over 600 000 km$^2$ of Amazon rainforest have been destroyed. In many tropical countries, most deforestation results from the actions of poor subsistence cultivators. However, in Brazil only about one-quarter of deforestation can be linked to small-scale farming, often of the 'shifting' variety (Figure 5.3). Typically, understory shrubbery is cleared and then forest trees are cut. The area is left to dry for a few months and then burned. The land is planted with crops such as bananas, palms, manioc, maize and rice. After a year or two the productivity of the soil declines, and the transient farmers press a little deeper and clear new forest for more short-term agricultural land. The old, now infertile fields are used for small-scale cattle-grazing or left for waste. Any recolonisation by secondary forest produces an ecosystem of much lower quality than that of the original forest.

**Figure 5.3**
*The main causes
of deforestation in
Brazil*

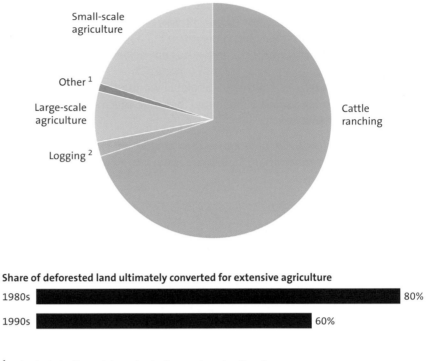

**Share of deforested land ultimately converted for extensive agriculture**

| | |
|---|---|
| 1980s | 80% |
| 1990s | 60% |

[1] Other includes fires, mining, urbanisation, road construction, dams
[2] Logging generally results in degradation rather than deforestation, but is often followed by clearing for
  agriculture

Historically, a large proportion (nearly three-quarters) of deforestation in Brazil can be attributed to the creation of huge cattle ranches. Much of the meat produced on these ranches is exported to Europe. In fact, little is consumed in Brazil. Nearly 10% of the deforestation is accounted for by large-scale commercial agriculture. Much of that land is being used to grow soya beans — another export crop. Soya beans are the primary ingredient in many processed foods, including dairy products and meat substitutes. Recently, forest has increasingly been cleared to grow palm oil, which fuel companies are now adding to diesel. This is part of the much broader move to substitute biofuels for fossil fuels (*Case study 47*).

What is noteworthy about Brazilian deforestation is that less than 5% is due to logging (the deliberate extraction of timber), much of it illegal. This small figure is explained, of course, by the fact that all the other commercial forms of deforestation inevitably produce a huge supply of hardwood timber for export.

It is extremely difficult to quantify the impact of all this deforestation on biodiversity. Over 600 species are recognised by the Brazilian government as being 'threatened', but no one really knows how many species have already been lost, such is the vastness of the Brazilian rainforests and the scientific ignorance of what they contain or once contained.

*Deforestation is a response to increased demands for farmland. It has serious consequences not only in terms of biodiversity loss and soil degradation, but also as a significant contributor to global warming.*

## 27 Question

Which human activity do you think poses the greatest threat to the Amazon rainforest? Give your reasons.

### Guidance

Start by looking at what Figure 5.3 tells you about the present 'consumers' of the forest. Is it possible to distinguish between them on the basis of lasting damage to the forest? Then anticipate how the pattern of consumers is likely to change. It would be helpful to take a look at *Case study 47*.

The major impact of food production occurs at the time when forest, wilderness or wetlands is initially cleared for cultivation. However, changes in farming practices themselves have been identified as causing declines in biodiversity, i.e. a serious reduction in the number of floral and faunal species. In the UK these include:

- concentration on winter crops, with a consequent loss of spring crops
- increased farm specialisation, with a decline in livestock and grass enterprises in arable areas
- changes in cultivation dates
- loss of semi-natural habitat in farmland, including field margins

# Landscape

So long is the history of food production, and so great its global distribution that its impact on the environment has been huge and extensive. In many parts of the world, the agricultural landscape is an integral part of heritage. Just look at a rural area near your home. What you might see includes:

- a patchwork of irregularly shaped fields that has not changed much over the last 250 years
- fields defined by hedgerows or stone walls of considerable age
- fields showing the ridge-and-furrow marks of the old open-field system and of early attempts to improve soil drainage
- a fairly regular network of farmhouses and farm buildings, some of which may well date back to the Middle Ages

Of course, the precise character of the agricultural landscape and its modification of the natural environment vary considerably from region to region, country to country and continent to continent. That character and that modification are also changing, subtly and slowly in some locations, dramatically in others.

Until the twentieth century, the evolution of the agricultural landscape involved a fairly benign form of environmental change. That has now altered quite dramatically. The villain of the piece in the developed world is technological progress (*Case study 32*), while in the less developed world it is population growth.

### The English experience

The adoption of a much more industrial approach to food production, plus the increasing presence of agribusiness in the whole food production business, has had a range of impacts on the English landscape:

- Field sizes have been increased to facilitate the use of larger machinery, leading to the loss of hedges and ditches as well as reducing the visual integrity of the landscape and the range of wildlife habitats.
- Hedgerows have declined in length and the botanical diversity of many field margins has also declined through nutrient enrichment and/or herbicide drift.
- Wetlands have been reclaimed and water formerly in ditches and streams has been piped underground.
- Woodlands, especially small copses, have been felled, and moorlands and heathlands have been ploughed up.
- Semi-natural grassland has declined as a result of being either ploughed up or converted into intensive grassland.
- The introduction of monoculture has reduced biodiversity and the variety of landscape patterns.
- Deeper ploughing and sub-soil operations have increased the potential for soil erosion and nutrient loss.
- The development of more intensive grassland through the use of higher inputs has produced a less visually harmonious landscape with jarring bright green swards.
- Increased stocking densities on upland grazing have resulted in sward damage and reduction or loss of species. This has also been encouraged by increased competition for grazing between domestic and wild species.
- Large-scale infrastructure items, such as grain silos, vast glasshouses, barns, livestock sheds and polytunnels are all potential eyesores (Figure 5.4).
- Leaching of nitrates from fertilisers has caused **eutrophication** of lakes, ponds and streams and the creation of algal blooms.

*Figure 5.4*
*Strawberries growing in polytunnels near Ivington in Herefordshire*

Andrew Fox/Alamy

Finally, remember that without agriculture, the landscape would take on a different appearance, often reverting over time to scrub and eventually woodland. This would smother the patterns and boundaries characteristic of the English landscape and diminish its scenic appeal.

*The modern landscape has been moulded by centuries of food production. Each advance in production makes a new impression. Given today's technology, landscape changes can be quite profound.*

## 28   Question

*Using case studies*

Of the 11 changes listed in the case study as impacting on the English landscape, which do you think is (a) most damaging scenically, (b) most damaging to biodiversity and (c) most beneficial to food production? Give your reasons.

### Guidance

(a) Depends on the beholder; (b) removal of hedgerows or woodland; (c) a close call.

# Water

Reference has already been made to some of food production's impacts on water resources — the depletion caused by over-pumping and salinisation (*Case study 30*). These are serious issues, and to them must be added pollution resulting from heavy use of fertilisers and pesticides (*Case study 33*).

## WATER POLLUTION IN THE PHILIPPINES

*Case study 33*

### The trouble with agrochemicals

It is estimated that 37% of water pollution in the Philippines as a whole originates from agricultural practices that include not only agrochemicals (fertilisers and pesticides) but also animal waste. Between 1961 and 2006, fertiliser applications in the Philippines increased by 1000%, and yields of rice and maize increased by 200% and 280% respectively. Between 1977 and 1987, pesticide use increased by 325%, but rice yields increased by only 30%.

According to a report produced by Greenpeace in 2008, water pollution from agrochemical runoff is much more widespread in the Philippines than previously thought. Recent studies show that excessive fertiliser use has already caused nitrate pollution in water bodies in agricultural areas in the country. Thirty per cent of the artesian wells tested in Benguet and Bulacan provinces were found to have nitrate levels above the World Health Organization (WHO) drinking water safety limit. Other recent studies found high levels of nitrates around sweet pepper farms in the Manguang area in Ilocos Norte. Nitrate pollution in water poses health risks, especially to children, and nitrogen-based fertiliser runoff has been identified as a cause of toxic algal blooms, such as red tide, in water bodies.

*There is a need in the Philippines and in many other parts of the world to reduce this high dependence on agrochemicals. Such dependence is having negative effects on human health, the environment and the economy of local communities. There are proven low-cost alternatives to the expensive chemical agriculture system (Case study 38).*

**29**

**Using case studies**

**Find out what nitrate-related diseases are likely to be experienced by children in the Philippines.**

**Guidance**

Visit: www.nitrate.com/nitrate3.htm

# Global warming (food miles)

As is the case in many developed countries, an increasing proportion of the UK's food supply is being transported over long distances. First it is moved from the fields to a storage facility, from there to a food processing plant, then to a packaging facility and finally to a supermarket near you. In some cases, food is even shipped across continents to be prepared or packaged, and then shipped back again for sale. In short, it is estimated that food travels on average 2400 km before its gets to the supermarket shelves. Consequently just over 10% of the average UK household's food-related greenhouse gas emissions come from transporting food. Food miles are a major consumer of non-renewable energy and a significant contributor to global warming. Are all these food miles really necessary?

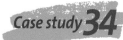 **Case study 34** UK FOOD MILES

### Fact file

- 1 kg of goods transported for 1 mile
  - by road: 0.2 MJ (megajoules)
  - by ship: 1.0 MJ
  - by air: 26.0 MJ
- Products travelling 5000 miles release 4500 g of greenhouse gas.
- See Table 5.1 for the mileage of common UK food imports.

Just think of the food miles and your contribution to global warming when you eat these foods!

**Table 5.1**
*UK food miles*

| Food | From | Distance |
|------|------|----------|
| Asparagus | Peru | 6000 miles |
| Pears | Argentina | 6500 miles |
| Carrots and peas | South Africa | 5900 miles |
| Chicken | Thailand | 6500 miles |
| Prawns | Indonesia | 7000 miles |
| Apples | California, USA | 5000 miles |
| Grapes | Chile | 7200 miles |
| Potatoes | Israel | 2200 miles |
| Tomatoes | Saudi Arabia | 3000 miles |
| Sprouts | Australia | 10000 miles |
| Lamb | New Zealand | 12000 miles |
| Sugar snap peas | Guatemala | 5000 miles |

## 30 Question

If you were a government official, which three imported foods listed in the case study would you totally ban? Give your reasons.

## Guidance

Your justification needs to be based on sound criteria, such as distance travelled, importance to a balanced diet, necessity of relying on foreign rather than UK producers etc.

# Drylands

This examination of the ways in which farming impacts on the environment concludes with a case study of desertification that involves all five environmental headings in Figure 5.1 (page 57). It is of special interest in that its causes are both natural (prolonged drought, wind) and human (overgrazing and overcultivation). In an era of global warming, no parts of the world seem more threatened than hot semi-arid and arid areas, the so called **drylands**. Life in these areas looks set to become even more marginal.

## THE SAHEL

*Case study* 35

### Desertification and food insecurity

The Sahel lies in northern Africa, south of the Sahara Desert but north of the Equator. Within it, countries such as Mauritania, Mali, Niger, Chad and Sudan are among the most food-insecure countries in the world. This part of Africa has for centuries been prone to devastating periods of drought. Typically, several years of abnormally low rainfall alternate with several successive years of average or above-average rainfall. But since the late 1960s, the periods of drought have become more frequent and persistent. Some say that this is due to climate change and quickly put the blame on global warming.

What is clear is that the Sahel region is the victim of desertification. This occurs during times of prolonged drought when human activities such as deforestation in the search for fuelwood, overgrazing by livestock, surface mining and poor irrigation techniques cause habitable land to be transformed into desert. In the case of the Sahel, desertification can largely be attributed to greatly increased numbers of people (overpopulation) and their grazing livestock. Most overgrazing is caused by excessive numbers of livestock feeding too long in a particular area. Extreme overgrazing compacts the soil and diminishes its capacity to hold water, and exposes it to erosion.

The relationship between natural drought and human influences is complex. This is well illustrated by the causal links in Figure 5.5. Particularly significant have been government programmes aimed at settling traditional nomads in designated areas, as well as expanding human and livestock populations. Perhaps the worst aspect of desertification is that it sets in motion a vicious downward spiral.

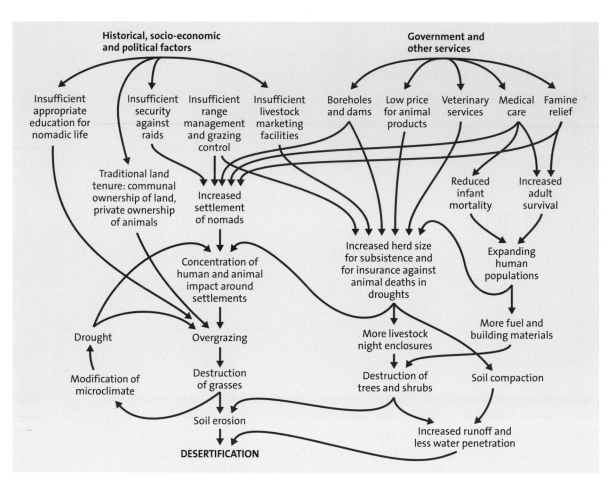

**Figure 5.5**
*Causes of
desertification*

So in the case of the Sahel, the path to greater food security and less environmental damage seems to lie in:

- reducing population numbers
- reducing livestock numbers
- investing in sustainable water supplies

*The serious food insecurity that prevails in the countries of the Sahel has its roots in a climate characterised by periods of drought that may be becoming more frequent and longer. But it is exacerbated by human-induced desertification, and in particular by food production and an overloaded carrying capacity (i.e. overpopulation).*

**31**

**Using case studies**

### Question

**Reread the six case studies in Part 5. Which do you think involves the most serious threat to the environment? Give your reasons.**

### Guidance

It will help if you establish on which criterion or criteria you are going to make your judgements: severity of impact, spatial scale of impact (i.e. how much of the world is likely to be affected), irreversibility etc.

The content of just six case studies carries serious warnings about the environmental costs associated with much of today's food production. It would be possible to cite many other adverse environmental impacts. It does seem that the world is fast approaching the critical threshold of a global catastrophe. The speed of approach is being accelerated by our need to feed the inevitable increase in the world's population. It would seem the only chance the world has to avoid this environmental Armageddon is to devise and apply more sustainable methods of food production, both in the developed and developing worlds. Possible methods are examined in the next part of the book.

# Strategies to increase food production and security in the developing world

A major challenge confronting the world is how to raise the level of food security both for today's citizens and for the increasing number of citizens expected over the next 50 years. The challenge may be met by taking action in three different but complementary directions, namely:

■ curbing the rate of population growth by voluntary means
■ ensuring that any food surpluses are moved to areas of food deficit
■ producing more food, but doing so in a sustainable way that does not inflict irreparable damage on the environment

The focus in this part of the book will be on the last line of action. We shall sample a range of possible actions that are expected to deliver an increased output of food, particularly in the developing world — actions that hopefully will reduce food availability deficits and food entitlement deficits.

We should start this discussion with some reference to the so-called Green Revolution. In the second half of the twentieth century, this did much to raise food production in LICs. However, as shown by Figure 6.1, the undoubted advances had a downside, particularly for:

■ the small subsistence farmer living close to the poverty line
■ the international trade of participating countries
■ the environment

In a word, there are aspects of the Green Revolution that made it unsustainable, but to be fair the Green Revolution was up and running long before the world became concerned about sustainability.

Recently, aspects of the Green Revolution have been taken up and modified to fit the circumstances prevailing over much of Africa. The outcomes promise to be

(+) The world is better off because there is far more food available from bigger harvests, than 20 years ago

(−) Bigger granaries storing more grain are not enough; hungry people need to be eating more; food in storage is not being distributed to the needy

(+) Significant and populous countries such as India, Indonesia and Thailand have become self-sufficient in basic foodstuffs; they are no longer dependent on North American and European food aid

(−) But implementing Green Revolution policies has increased dependency on imported seeds, fertilisers, pesticides and farm machinery

(+) Former food importers such as India and Thailand now export grain, earning useful foreign exchange; initially the taste of HYV rice products was a problem

(−) Imports of seeds, petrochemical fertilisers and fuel for machinery all cost valuable foreign exchange, and give control to agrochemical multinationals

(+) New farming methods with irrigation can bring all-year-round employment; no longer do workers have to be laid off in the dry season; double cropping is common

(−) Often, agricultural profits are invested in tractors, which reduce employment

(+) (−)

**Assessment**

Increasing food production does not stem hunger on its own. It is possible to have both more food and more hunger. 'If the poor don't have money to buy food,' a World Bank report said, 'increased production won't help them.' Nevertheless, increasing harvests by 30% is the equivalent of discovering 30% more farming land — and as the population is increasing, that is a welcome relief.

(+) The environmental impact of impoverished rural people — who cut down trees — is lessened by urban migration

(−) New farming methods can bring an increase in water-borne diseases (with irrigation), the development of 'super-pests' (resistant to insecticides), and desertification (through the salinisation of waterlogged fields); increased fertiliser use leads to eutrophication; biodiversity is lost as native breeds are replaced by high-yielding varieties (HYVs)

(+) With bigger harvests, farmers earn more and the price of food stays constant or even becomes cheaper in the marketplace

(−) For the small farmers who cannot afford the Green Revolution seeds and other technology, the lower prices for their harvests means real hardship — often they have to sell off to the big landowners, bringing an increasing gap between rich and poor

distinctly 'greener'. For examples, visit the following websites:
www.agra-alliance.org
www.africangreenrevolution.com
www.rockfound.org/library/africas_turn.pdf

What about the Green Revolution's successor — the **Gene Revolution**?

***Figure 6.1***
*Benefits and costs of the Green Revolution*

# The Gene Revolution

There is nothing new in trying to improve both crops and livestock. Selective plant and animal breeding has been undertaken for centuries. However, modern bio-technology is now capable of altering the DNA of crops (and presumably livestock). Initially, the aim was to produce GM crops with higher yields and a better resistance to pests and pesticides. This we might see as the GM Revolution (Part 1). More recently, research has turned to producing plants that will be better able to flourish in the harsher environmental conditions associated with global warming, namely plants with a greater tolerance of drought and soil salinity. These challenges are particularly significant given that many of the world's food-insecure areas are in semi-arid locations experiencing desertification and/or salinisation. But perhaps the most exciting development of the GM Revolution (Part 2) is promoting the trait called nitrogen-use efficiency.

Over much of the world, crop yields rely heavily on large amounts of nitrogen fertiliser, the manufacture of which emits vast amounts of carbon dioxide (1% of all greenhouse gas emissions). Most crops take up less than half of the nitrogen that is supplied in the fertiliser, and the excess simply contaminates the soil, the runoff and groundwater. Worse still, nitrates in the soil can be converted into nitrous oxide, a greenhouse gas that is 300 times as potent as carbon dioxide. But improving the efficiency with which plants use the available nitrogen means fertiliser applications can be greatly reduced, and so too the emission of greenhouse gases.

Currently, there is much optimism about the ability of GM crops (Part 2) to raise food production and increase food security in the developing world (*Case study 36*).

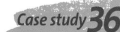

## Case study 36 — GM CROPS AND THE DEVELOPING WORLD

### Possible benefits and concerns

The Nuffield Council on Bioethics has suggested that GM crops could provide solutions to problems that currently afflict developing countries and significantly reduce crop yields, including:

- insect/pest resistance — by introducing a substance that is poisonous to the particular pest or insect
- disease resistance — by genetically modifying plants to make them resistant to bacterial, fungal or viral infestation
- crops that can withstand environmental stresses such as drought, heat, frost, acid or salty soils
- herbicide tolerance — by genetically modifying plants to be tolerant of a specific weedkiller
- reduced use of fertiliser
- improved nutritional value — by modifying crops so that they contain additional nutrients that are lacking in the diets of many people (e.g. β-carotene)
- biopharmaceuticals — modifying plants to produce vaccines or other medicines

The growing of GM crops is being held back by a number of key questions that have yet to be answered in a definitive and reassuring way:

- Are GM crops safe to eat? Some people feel that the effects on human health are not yet adequately understood. However, the current evidence from safety assessments of GM crops does not suggest any significant risks to people who eat them.
- What are the environmental risks of introducing GM crops in developing countries? There are concerns that the introduction of GM crops might 'contaminate' neighbouring crops (particularly those of organic farmers) and lead to a reduction in biodiversity. There is also the risk of gene transfer between plants, as for example the 'escape' of genes into neighbouring wild plants via pollen. Pests and weeds could acquire the same resistances as those inbred in GM crops (Figure 6.2).
- Should there be concern about the corporate control of GM crops? Five biotechnological TNCs now control most of the technology needed to develop GM crops, as well as the agrochemicals and crop **genome** (tissue from which new plants can be grown). It does appear that these companies which own the intellectual property rights have undue influence over the availability of GM crops. Equally, it is conceded that these companies need to recoup their considerable research and development costs. It also

PeerPoint/Alamy

needs to be understood that much of GM research currently only serves the interests of large-scale farmers in developed countries. What is still needed is a major expansion of GM-related research relevant to the needs of small-scale, largely subsistence farmers in developing countries.

Finally, it needs to be pointed out that biotechnology has largely been focused on the genetic modification of cotton, rice, maize and soya bean. However, the basic foods of the poor in the developing world, such as cassava, millet, sorghum, tef, potato and wheat, have so far received little attention.

**Figure 6.2**
*Activists against genetically modified crops tearing up plants at a GM test crop site in Oxfordshire*

**32**

*Using case studies*

### Question

**Which of the two revolutions do you think offers LICs a more sustainable food supply? Give your reasons.**

### Guidance

You need to have a sound grasp of the meaning of sustainability and would be advised to focus on such aspects as access to the required technology, environmental conditions and the nature of subsistence farming.

It seems that while the Gene Revolution promises an increased food supply, it cannot be wholly embraced by the developing world — or not yet, at least. There are economic, social and technological gaps to be bridged. Equally, there is much concern in the developed world about the possible repercussions of growing GM crops (*Case studies 36 and 46*).

*Food & Famine*

# Sustainable options

## Diversifying the crop base

We noted in *Case study 36* that the Gene Revolution has yet to do much for many of the staple foods consumed in the developing world. That being the case, perhaps it would be more prudent to explore whether the food situation might be improved not by using GM technologies but by growing a wider diversity of staple crops known to flourish in tropical areas — for example, roots and tubers such as cassava, yams and taro. They are all nutritious foods, high in carbohydrates, calcium and vitamin C. Moreover, they are easily grown, even on poor soils.

A closely allied strategy would be to examine the food histories of traditional subsistence societies. Are there any staple crops that have fallen out of cultivation that might be resurrected? *Case study 37* considers two neglected staples in Latin America that could easily be cultivated in similar parts of the world faced with food insecurity.

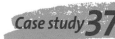

## Case study 37 — TWO FORGOTTEN CROPS IN LATIN AMERICA

**Figure 6.3**
*(a) Amaranth*
*(b) Quinoa*

Of the many food crops that have largely passed into history, there are two that deserve to be resurrected because of their considerable food value and the fact that they could flourish in areas currently suffering from food insecurity.

### Amaranth

Amaranth is a remarkable plant on a number of counts. It can be cooked as a cereal to make a sort of gruel, ground into flour, popped like popcorn, sprouted or toasted. The seeds can be cooked with other whole grains, and added to stir-fry or to soups and stews as a nutrient-rich thickening agent. The seeds can also be fermented to make a kind of beer, and its leaves boiled or fried and eaten as a vegetable. In some traditional societies it is used medicinally to treat toothache and fever. It is also an attractive plant, its flowers being used for decorative purposes.

The plant is an annual herb, not a 'true' grain, and is a relative of pigweed, a common wild plant. It is a bushy plant that grows to a height of between 1 and 2 metres. Each plant is capable of producing 40 000 to 60 000 seeds. Not only is amaranth a diverse source of food, it is extremely adaptable to adverse growing conditions. It resists heat and drought, has no major disease problems, and is among the easiest of plants to grow. Simply scratching the soil, throwing down some seeds and watering will be rewarded with a fast-growing and highly useful plant.

Once a staple in the diets of pre-Columbian societies in Central and South America, it is cultivated today in only a few scattered locations in Mexico, Peru and, surprisingly, Nepal. So why is this useful plant largely ignored today? Before the Spanish conquests, amaranth was associated with religious ceremonies and human sacrifices. For this reason, its cultivation was banned and perhaps by default that ban has remained fairly effective to this day.

There is no doubt that amaranth could play a significant part in the fight against food insecurity.

## Quinoa

The quinoa is a leafy herb that grows up to 2 metres tall and produces an amazing abundance of seeds that can be made into various forms of food. The plant will grow in the toughest of environments — for example, it is known to flourish in the arid areas of the high Andes. Farmers simply have to dig a hole in the ground with a spear-like instrument and drop in the seed. Within months and with a minimum of care the quinoa will mature. At harvest time the plants are uprooted from the soil, then dried in the sun and threshed by hand. The seeds can now be stored for years without spoiling. During the long dry season in the Andes, it is a staple food that the people are fully reliant on.

Quinoa is consumed in various forms — as a breakfast cereal and as a flour made into bread, biscuits or tortillas. Nutritionists have discovered that quinoa is low in sugar and starch and high in fibre and unsaturated fats. It contains many essential vitamins and minerals. What has the experts most excited, however, is the amount of protein in quinoa. It contains 50% more protein than wheat, rice and barley, and the protein is of superior quality. It contains an ideal balance of the amino acids needed by the human body, including lysine, which is rarely found in vegetable protein and normally only found in meat, fish and eggs. Quinoa is also a good source of phosphorous, calcium, iron, vitamin E and several of the B vitamins.

Like amaranth, quinoa came to the attention of the Spanish *conquistadores*, but in this case they were inclined to ignore it as a cheap food fit only for peasants. Like amaranth, however, quinoa has the potential to raise levels of food security in physically difficult areas. Its widespread growth would not only deliver food to fill empty stomachs, but provide food with a remarkable nutritional balance.

So is it not about time that both governmental and non-governmental organisations concerned with food security started to promote these two forgotten crops in a big way?

**33** **Using case studies**

**Imagine you have been given the task of promoting the cultivation of quinoa in Bolivia, a country suffering from food insecurity. What points would you make to 'sell' the idea?**

### Guidance

Reread the case study and research the particular conditions that prevail in Bolivia. Visit: **www.worldbank.org** and **www.cia.org/Cia_World_Factbook**

# Permaculture

A second possible pathway to increased food security may again involve revisiting the old farming practices, but this time looking for lapsed farming methods rather than abandoned food crops. Were there old methods of farming that had a more harmonious relationship with the environment? This question is partly what led to the development of an organic method of farming (**permaculture**) that is beginning to be taken up in many parts of the world (*Case study 38*).

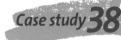

## Case study 38  PERMACULTURE

### Making the best use of nature, from Canada to Cuba

When trying to increase the output of food, it makes sense to use what the natural world provides in the best possible ways. That is the ethos of permaculture (permanent cultivation). Permaculture is a method of producing foodstuffs in a closed loop that maintains a self-sufficient system. In any habitat, animals, plants and microorganisms work together in harmony.

Although first developed in Australia in the late 1970s, the technique really began to take off only in the 1990s. Permaculture is knowledge-intensive, so training is needed. There are now over 100 permaculture training institutes in the developing world.

In permaculture, farmers use no inputs, such as chemicals or pesticides, from outside the area where they farm. They grow a mixture of food and tree crops, and often keep a small number of livestock, with each part of the system benefiting from the other parts. For example, livestock (notably chickens) are allowed to forage after crops have been harvested, and in return provide manure. Trees are planted around the fields and these soon produce mulch and nitrogen — natural fertilisers that are washed into the fields by rain. Often fruit and vegetables are among the trees. Indigenous trees are preferred, because part of the permaculture technique involves making insecticide sprays from their leaves, bark and wood. All the trees and crops are in a form of symbiotic relationship, the idea being to balance sunlight and shade, pests and predators. The soil is never left exposed to the sun and wind: it is heavily mulched to keep it cool and damp. As one farmer has put it, 'All plants, insects, animals and we who tend the garden live in a natural harmony'.

Experience has shown that permaculture can be adapted to work well in both humid and arid environments. In the latter, training courses provide instruction in simple but effective water conservation techniques. In most cases, farmers can expect to increase their yields from upwards of four times within a few years. Besides delivering food security, the system allows farmers to reduce the proportion of their land used for immediate subsistence needs. Thus they have an opportunity to raise a cash crop or two.

There are permaculture ventures now up and running in all the continents, and they are not just confined to developing countries. Indeed, there is much enthusiasm for the concept in Canada, the USA and Australia. Cuba is one country that has very successfully embraced the concept. A long-standing trade embargo imposed on Cuba by the USA, plus the collapse of the island's sugar exports to the former Soviet Union, triggered the switch to low-input organic farming. With no access to the chemicals and machinery needed for modern intensive agriculture, it had no other option. But Cuba has taken the permaculture idea a step further by demonstrating that it can be made

**Figure 6.4**
Urban gardens in
Havana

Fabienne Fossez/Alamy

to work well in an urban environment. Urban gardens in Havana, ranging in size from a few square metres to a few hectares, now produce about half of the capital city's food supply (Figure 6.4). Thanks to Cuba's adaptation of permaculture, food production in the country as a whole has increased significantly. Cuba is beginning to enjoy an increasing measure of food security.

For a comparable development in HICs, see *Case study 44*).

*The principles of permaculture can be applied in a wide range of natural environments. Its other attractions are that it is environmentally friendly, it only requires* **intermediate technology**, *it is sustainable and it provides food security.*

## Aquaculture

The sea and freshwater resources of the world have always been a source of food for people. The question now is, can these waters provide more food to help the drive to food security? It is tempting to respond in a negative way, bearing in mind the much-publicised depletion of fish stocks in large oceanic areas. In the UK we are only too aware of, for example, the loss of herring from the North Sea and of cod from the North Atlantic. The EU's fishing quotas represent a last-ditch attempt to avert the extinction of fish species that have been important sources of food.

### GLOBAL AQUACULTURE

*Case study* **39**

#### Fact file

- During the past three decades, the number of fishermen and fish farmers has grown faster than the world's population, and employment in the fisheries sector has grown faster than employment in traditional agriculture.
- The great majority of fishers and fish farmers are in developing countries, principally in Asia.

- The contribution of **aquaculture** to global supplies of fish, crustaceans, molluscs and other aquatic animals continues to grow, increasing from roughly 4% of total production by weight in 1970 to around 33% in 2009.
- Aquaculture continues to grow more rapidly than all other animal food-producing sectors. Worldwide, the sector has grown at an average rate of 8.8% per year since 1970, compared with only 2.8% for terrestrial farmed meat production systems over the same period.

Production from aquaculture has greatly outpaced population growth, with per capita supply from aquaculture increasing from 0.7 kg in 1970 to 7.1 kg in 2009, representing an average annual growth rate of 7.1%.

World aquaculture (food fish and aquatic plants) has grown significantly during the past half-century. From a total of below 1 million tons in the early 1950s, production has now risen to over 60 million tons.

Countries in Asia and the Pacific region account for just over 90% of the production quantity and 80% of the value. China is reported to account for 70% of the quantity, and just over 50% of the total value, of global aquaculture production.

There are also concerns about the sustainability of aquaculture. From the fish-ponds of China to the fish farms of Scotland there are reports of waters becoming seriously polluted by feedstuffs and by chemicals used to reduce the incidence of fish diseases.

*Aquaculture has a greater role to play in raising global food production. However, its contribution in the drylands of the world is likely to be very modest, other than in those states possessing a coast. Its impact on water environments seriously undermines its potential sustainability.*

Perhaps the most surprising fact to emerge is that the food-security benefits of aquaculture are only really being exploited in Asia. While not all countries have coastal waters, the great majority do have watercourses or are capable of excavating fish ponds and tanks. So why is aquaculture not being promoted much more in the hungry countries of Africa? There are some risks to do with environmental pollution, food safety and public health, but surely these are outweighed by the considerable potential of aquaculture to supplement food supplies in a sustainable way?

## Water conservation

In the past, irrigation has been seen as playing an important part in raising food production. But most forms of irrigation are far from efficient — much water is lost, which deprives plants of the maximum benefit. In an era of global warming and increasing desertification, the availability of adequate water supplies is going to be a critical element in the food security formula. If it is conceivable that countries will come to blows over food supplies in the near future, it looks even more likely that it will happen over water. Effective and inexpensive water conservation techniques are urgently needed in areas of marginal water supplies. Remember that about 70% of the freshwater used in the world is consumed by food production.

## BASIC WATER CONSERVATION

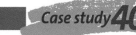
### Some simple techniques

Improving the efficiency with which water is used is crucial to improved food production in hot arid and semi-arid areas. Water is lost in four ways: evaporation, transpiration, runoff and percolation (Figure 6.5).

- **Evaporation** — the longer water remains on or near the surface, the more is lost through evaporation. Clayey soils keep water at or near the surface because infiltration rates are slow. Adding organic matter and sand can improve porosity and infiltration rates and thereby reduce loss through evaporation. Organic matter can be obtained through composting the inedible parts of crops and by making use of human waste.

- **Transpiration** — high temperatures, long sunshine hours and drying winds mean that losses of water vapour from crop plants can be very high. Such losses can be reduced by using the shade provided by more permanent vegetation such as trees and bushes, or by windbreaks. In Egypt, for example, young tender seedlings are protected from drying winds and wind-borne sand by careful placement of maize or wheat stalks just upwind of the seedlings. Mixed plantings of crops of different forms and life cycles can reduce both evaporation and transpiration.

- **Runoff** — water from direct rainfall or irrigation may reach a crop, but if not contained it can so easily run off and be of no use. Planting crops in sunken beds or depressions is a long tradition in many societies and areas, from the Native Americans in the southwest USA to tribes in west Africa. This is a simple and effective way to contain and concentrate water in the cultivated area. Another advantage is that soil is less likely to be washed away by sudden heavy rainfall.

- **Percolation** — once water has passed through the root zone of crops, it is lost. But such deep percolation is needed in order to wash salts out of the root zone, otherwise

**Figure 6.5**
*Simplified diagram of the hydrological cycle*

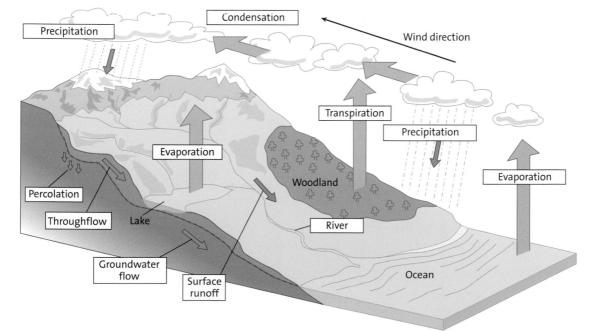

salinisation (*Case study 30*) becomes a problem. So the challenge here is one of achieving a balance — to restrain percolation by adding organic matter to the root zone and at the same time to allow a certain amount of water to do the necessary flushing out of unwanted salts.

Of course, if the water conservation actions just described were to be too effective, it is possible that they might seriously disrupt the hydrological cycle and ultimately reduce rainfall to even lower levels.

*The art of water conservation advocated here is one of retaining water longer and thereby allowing more to be 'squeezed' out of it for food production purposes. Not only that, but the techniques involved do not require high-tech inputs.*

Meanwhile, research in the UK is producing a cultivation technique that may halve the water consumption of crops and yet raise nutritional values. So far, this water rationing technique has only been applied to the growing of strawberries. The hope is that the technique will eventually 'bear fruit' with respect to staple food crops. In the meantime, there are now some fairly efficient irrigation techniques available, such as **drip irrigation**. But these, too, require access to quite sophisticated technology.

**34** **Using case studies**

### Question

**Which of the four options (diversifying the crop base, permaculture, aquaculture, water conservation) do you think holds out most promise in terms of raising food production in the world's drylands? What criteria would you use to assess their sustainability?**

### Guidance

You need to constantly remind yourself of the context — hot arid and semi-arid climates. Will all the four options work equally well in such environmental conditions?
Visit: **www.drylandsresearch.org.uk**

Possible criteria: greenness, futurity, pro-poor, bottom-up.

All but one of the options discussed above would seem to offer hope to those areas of the world that are most in need of more food and more food security — the hot semi-arid and arid locations. Only the greatest optimist would suggest that aquaculture might play some part!

# Broad approaches

The way forward for those parts of the world most in need of food is not going to be achieved by any one single action. Certainly there is scope for combining some if not all of the four actions just discussed. These actions are very direct ways of achieving a more secure food supply by what could promise to be sustainable pathways. But there are other possible routes. Some of them are much broader in nature and involve fundamental changes to society. They are less directly concerned with food production: it would be more accurate to say that their aim is to achieve a

sustainable balance between people and resources. *Case study 41* considers four possible pathways.

## FOOD PRODUCTION AND CONSUMPTION

### Four alternative pathways

The remit of this book is a focus on food production and food security. Apart from ways of increasing the global output of food, there are alternative courses of action that might help reduce the mismatch between food consumption and production. Some are fairly obvious and direct, others are less so. In this case study, we highlight a sample of four.

### *Population control*

It is widely recognised that population numbers are a major factor in food security. Some argue that the apparently close association between overpopulation and food insecurity means that the control of population growth and population distribution would be obvious courses of action to take. However, this may be easier said than done. While there are governments that actively promote the use of contraceptives, few governments have ever attempted to manage the distribution of people. But even with the former, young women's use of modern methods of contraception is limited by a range of factors. This was the conclusion of studies conducted in five developing countries. Lack of knowledge, access problems and side-effect fears were the factors limiting the women's use of hormonal contraceptives such as the birth control pill or hormone implants. In addition, there are factors associated with cultural traditions. For example, young women said they were reluctant to use modern contraceptive methods because they perceived them as intended for married women. Many women also feared having others find out that they were using contraceptives, because they would be known to be having sex, or thought of as being unable to bear children later on.

Sadly, the factor that seems to be having the greatest impact on population rates of growth in the developing world is the spread of HIV/AIDS. Erosion of the number of people in the reproductive age range has resulted in reduced birth rates.

### *Gender equality*

It is estimated that women farmers produce a large proportion of the world's food — between 80 and 90% in sub-Saharan Africa, 50 to 90% in Asia and 30% in eastern Europe. As an FAO official has put it, 'There would be no food security without rural women'.

Despite the importance of food production to survival, in many countries farming is regarded as inferior work. For that reason it is left for women to do, as part of their lot as second-class citizens. Two-thirds of the world's illiterate people are female.

Giving women equal access to education would enable them to be more aware of techniques that could help them to raise the levels of food production and food security. Keeping women illiterate and ignorant does no one any good — not even the domineering and exploitative males.

### *Fairer trade*

Liberalising global trade would improve the flow of food from areas with food surpluses to those with food deficits. Also, fair trade would allow agricultural produce from developing countries easier access to the lucrative markets of the developed world. But pause for a moment: would such a development

necessarily benefit the food producers? It is questionable. Earlier case studies have indicated that the commercialisation of agriculture in developing countries has the backlash effect of reducing subsistence farming and generally raising the price of staple foods (*Case studies 2 and 3*). That is certainly the case if commercial agriculture is in the hands of agribusinesses (*Case study 25*).

### Appropriate aid

When it comes to helping developing countries, what is important is not so much the amount of aid that is given, but rather the form it takes.

- Aid in the form of food is fine in disaster and emergency situations, such as during a famine. However, giving such aid during more 'normal' times can only create an unwanted level of dependence. In virtually all cases, it is better to be producing food than relying on handouts.
- Outside emergency situations, aid in the form of technical assistance is best. In the context of improving food security, this might involve helping local agriculture with seeds, stock, tools and instruction about the techniques of sustainable farming (*Case studies 38 and 40*). It might also involve setting up local cooperatives and market groups and generally giving local communities the know-how and confidence to help themselves. The aid needs to rely on intermediate, rather than high, technology. The work of Farm-Africa has been exemplary in this respect.
- 'Tied aid', like loans, is an inappropriate form of aid. Tied aid involves an agreement between the donor country and the receiving country that in return for food aid the latter will purchase something made in the former (manufactured goods, armaments etc.). The terms of tied aid invariably favour the donor.
  Research the following websites:
  www.practicalaction.org
  www.oxfam.org.uk/oxfam_in_action/issues/global_food_crisis.html

*None of the four options considered here provides a fast route to food security. In theory, population control has the greatest potential to improve situations. In practice, perhaps gender equality and appropriate aid are likely to have a favourable impact. For all the hype about the desirability of fairer trade, it does have a downside — increasing food entitlement deficits.*

**35** Using case studies

## Question

**Which of the four actions discussed in *Case study 41* do you think is most likely to achieve a sustainable balance between population and resources? Give your reasons.**

## Guidance

Each action needs to be evaluated in two ways. Which one on its own should, in theory, have the greatest potential impact? Which one is most likely to be implemented? An initial reaction might be to go for population control, but take a longer cool look at the other three.

# Issues relating to food security and sustainability

An alien visiting today's world would be intrigued to notice what a divided and illogical planet it is. Roughly half of the Earth's land surface is occupied by people who have more than enough food to eat and who are also capable of producing more food than they can possibly eat. The other half is occupied by people who suffer varying degrees of hunger and who at the moment are unable to produce sufficient food. To an outsider, the simple solution to this global situation would be to find ways of moving the food surplus from the one half to feed the hungry in the other half. But what does our alien discover? That the hungry half, rather than trying to feed itself rather better, is now growing 'luxury' food for the benefit of the other half. These humans are crazy! And if the alien understood about food miles (*Case study 34*), the global situation would look even more silly.

That craziness perhaps extends further in that the hungry half of the world is now expected not only to grow food for others but also to grow produce for biofuels that will mainly be burnt in the other half of the world. So in this part of the book we will draw attention to a number of issues that are in a sense getting in the way of reducing food availability and food entitlement deficits (FADs and FEDs) in the developing world and of moving towards more sustainable modes of food production.

## Only an LIC problem?

There is a tendency in the UK and other HICs to think that food security is a challenge that confronts only LICs. Perhaps the content of Part 6 has encouraged you to think in this way. The next case study should drive home the point that even in a country with no FADs and only small pockets of FEDs there is concern about future food security.

## The UK's view of its own future food security

You might be thinking that the UK is one of the last nations that should be worried by food security. But although the UK's food supply is currently secure, population growth and climate are recognised as having the potential to alter that situation fairly swiftly. Thus in 2009 the government published a consultation document entitled *Food 2030*. This attempted to identify the actions that should be taken to ensure the country's food security over the next two decades, particularly in the light of what is happening to the global food situation.

The main warning lights prompting this consultation were:

■ the surge in global food prices following events in 2007–08 — the global recession and the sudden hike in oil prices
■ the declining level in the UK's self-sufficiency in food production — we now import 40% of our food, 20% of it coming from Europe (Figures 7.1 and 7.2)

**Figure 7.1**
*UK food self-sufficiency, 1980–2005 (100% = self-sufficiency threshold)*

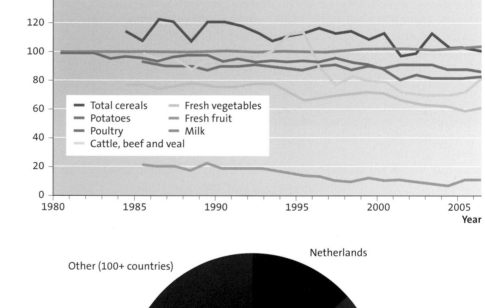

**Figure 7.2**
*Where the UK gets its food*

- global uncertainties (population growth, climate change, geopolitics etc.) that could so easily cut off supplies of imported food

To its credit, *Food 2030* recognises the complexities of food production and supply. In this vein, it seeks to consult with everyone involved in the food supply chain, from the farmer to the consumer, and in between stakeholders such as the food processors, the distributors and the retailers.

To initiate the discussion, the consultation document suggests a range of possible actions (some quite controversial) to be taken to ensure the UK's continuing food security. At the producer end of the food supply chain, a number of actions are suggested:

- To grow still more food per hectare, but in a sustainable way that uses less energy and water per unit of output. That might sound like an impossible challenge, but researchers believe that we have the requisite technology already.
- To persuade the public that GM crops have a vital part to play in raising crop yields, not just in the UK and other HICs but also in the developing world.
- For the food processing industry to reduce the amount of packaging, particularly 'tempting' packaging that encourages consumers to overbuy.

At the consumer end of the food supply chain, appropriate actions are no less significant:

- To eliminate the large amount of food wasted every year. It is estimated that around one-third of the food we buy every year ends up in the dustbin. The value of average annual household food waste in the UK is £420. Criticism has been aimed at the supermarkets and their 'bogof' (buy one, get one free) and 'loss leader' promotions that encourage shoppers to buy more food than they need.
- To tackle diet-related ill health that already costs the NHS and the economy billions of pounds each year. Basically the message is: 'Eat less and eat sensibly'.

*Food 2030 is to be applauded for taking into account the whole of the food supply chain rather than just one component. This wider approach is more likely to achieve the ultimate aim of a more self-sufficient and food-secure UK. The apparent awareness of the need for sustainability is also encouraging.*

**36** **Question**
**Write an essay explaining why it is imperative that the UK reduces its imports of food.**

**Guidance**
Identify those aspects of food imports that reduce the country's food security.

*Using case studies*

When it comes to what we as individuals can do in the UK to make our lifestyles more sustainable, there are a number of actions that we might take. The next two case studies illustrate just two of these.

It is ironic that at both ends of the food–famine continuum there are dietary problems: malnutrition and emaciation at one end and overnutrition and obesity at the other (Figure 1.12, page 15). But successful progress in terms of economic development does not necessarily mean that a nation's population should always take the fast track to obesity and early death. The case of Japan stands as a shining example to all the developed countries of the world (*Case study 43*). It suggests we should think more in terms of sustainable diets.

## Case study 43  EATING THE JAPANESE WAY

### An example for the heavy eaters to follow

Thanks to a relatively healthy diet, Japanese men and women live longer and enjoy healthier lives. Not only can they expect to live 79 and 86 years respectively (compared with 77 and 81 years for Britons and 75 and 80 years for Americans), but also they enjoy the lowest obesity rate in the developed world — 3%, compared with 19% for the UK and 32% for the USA. So what is so special about the Japanese diet?

- The Japanese person eats 25% fewer calories per day than the average American. The secret is that the Japanese consume very small amounts of the energy-dense foods (chocolate, crisps, biscuits and sweetened drinks), but far more of the less energy-dense foods, such as fruit, vegetables, soups and green tea.
- The typical diet features little by way of meat, dairy products and bread. Instead, it contains more fish and seafood, rice, noodles and soya (tofu and miso). When beef and chicken are served, they are regarded as 'side dishes' rather than as the main focus of the meal.
- Food is often eaten from separate small bowls and plates instead of on one big plate. This encourages people to eat generally smaller portions.
- The Japanese 'eat with their eyes' by enjoying the beauty of the food they eat (Figure 7.3). A great deal of emphasis is placed on presentation and making the food

*Figure 7.3*
*The Japanese enjoy the beauty of the food they eat — the emphasis is on presentation and making the food look appealing*

Leonid Nyshko/Fotolia

look beautiful and appealing to the eye. This might sound rather fanciful but the outcome is a practical and beneficial one. The Japanese eat at a slow rate and this gives the brain time to realise when it has eaten enough. A major feature of their way of eating is to eat until '80% full'.

■ Breakfast is considered the most important meal of the day and is often the largest. This means that calories are burnt off during the working day rather than being left to turn to fat when consumed late in the day.

*So the Japanese diet delivers a triple whammy of relatively good health, long life and a modest drain on global food resources.*

**37** **Using case studies**

## Question

**Which of the bulleted points in the case study do you think is the most important? Give your reasons.**

## Guidance

The answer depends on your key criterion — food security, health or environment.

There is one aspect of changing diet that could bring benefits to both global food production and human health. Shifting towards a more vegetarian diet in the developed world and persuading developing countries that economic success does not require them to consume more meat and dairy products would be two powerful moves to more sustainable diets. It is important to realise that one-third of the world's grain production is fed to animals. In developed countries that figure rises to 60%, and in the USA it is 80%. Table 7.1 makes the point that meat production is an extravagant use of food that might otherwise be fed to humans.

**Table 7.1** *The grain consumption of meat production*

| Meat | Kg of grain to produce 1 kg of meat |
|------|-------------------------------------|
| Lamb | 16 |
| Beef | 10 |
| Pork | 4 |
| Chicken | 2 |

There are two other points to remember:

■ Livestock is a major producer of methane, one of the greenhouse gases contributing to global warming.
■ The consumption of meat and dairy products carries with it some serious health risks.

Despite all this, present levels of meat and milk production are expected to double by 2050. Many people argue that it would be better to reduce livestock numbers and use the grain to feed hungry people instead of animals for the meat market.

Finally, a quick reference to an aspect of diet that has some bearing on the whole sustainability issue. This is the rising consumption of so-called 'organic' food in the developed world. *Case study 44* shows that organic farming is possibly more sustainable in terms of both the environment and human health. The latter view was challenged in 2009 by a UK Food Standards Agency report which concluded that in terms of nutrition content and additional health benefits there was no important difference between organic food and conventionally produced food. (It did not address the issue of the contaminating effect of pesticides, herbicides and chemical fertilisers on both.) The report did not, however, go so far as to claim that buying organic food was a waste of money.

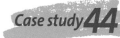

## Case study 44 GOING ORGANIC

### Well worth it?

Despite its higher prices, an increasing number of us are buying food that merits the Soil Association's 'organic' label. Over the last 5 years, sales of organic food have nearly doubled to about £2 billion. Our motivations for buying such food from farmers' markets, health food shops and designated sections in our supermarkets range from believing that it is healthier and better for us, to feeling that organic farming is kinder to animals and to the environment. We can be fairly sure that organic produce does not contain pesticides and chemicals that can harm our health and the environment, particularly its ecosystems.

**Figure 7.4**
*The organic shopping basket in the UK*

■ Dairy products
■ Fresh fruit & veg
■ Other
□ Meat
▨ Beverages
▨ Clothes
■ Cosmetics

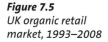

Most people believe that organic farming helps to promote local seasonal foods and reduce food miles. Buying organic produce is also thought to support the rural economy and, in particular, smaller food producers. In 2008 the Soil Association (the watchdog of organic food production in the UK) proposed to ban suppliers and retailers from putting its certification label on fruit and vegetables that arrived in the UK by air. It argued that air-freighting produce generated 177 times more greenhouse gases than sending the same produce by sea, and infinitely more than producing it in the UK. But the Soil Association was forced

**Figure 7.5**
*UK organic retail market, 1993–2008*

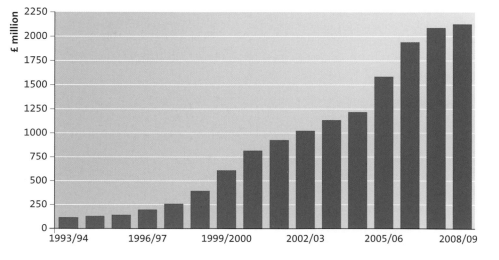

to yield to the big supermarkets' desire to continue selling air-freighted organic food. The excuse made was that many African 'farmers' (more likely agribusinesses or the 'expats' who control the trading) depended on air freight to get their produce to the UK market in prime condition. But many supporters of the organic lifestyle believe that it should stand for sustainable consumption, not just organic production.

One early victim of the credit crunch in 2007–09 was expected to be sales of organic food (Figure 7.5). The Soil Association estimated that annual growth in sales of organic food would fall to 5% compared with a rate of 30% in earlier years. It seemed that people who bought organic for ethical reasons were settling for fairtrade products rather than local organic food.

An important postscript is that the selling of locally produced organic foods through farmers' markets and farm shops can dramatically reduce food miles. That is good for the global environment, but perhaps not so good for those producers in LICs exporting food to HIC supermarkets.

Research: **www.soilassociation.org**

*There is a growing body of support for organic food on the grounds that it is kind to the environment and to the human body.*

---

**38**
**Using case studies**

### Question

Study Figure 7.5. Suggest reasons why the growth in UK organic retail sales appeared to be levelling off prior to 2008.

### Guidance

Is everyone sold on the idea of eating organic food?

---

## A SOIL STRATEGY FOR THE UK

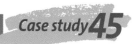
*Case study* **45**

### Cutting-edge food production

The soil is the biggest carbon store after the oceans. Ploughing releases some of that carbon. It is partly for this reason that in September 2009 the UK government launched a 'soil strategy'. Farmers are to be encouraged to adopt 'no tilling and low tilling' techniques that will reduce the environmental impact of food production, particularly greenhouse gas emissions. 'Precision farming' involves investing in machines that do not deep-plough the soil. Rather, the equipment merely turns over the top layer and seed is planted on the soil that includes the stubble from the previous crop. The soil fabric remains relatively undisturbed. The new machinery also prevents over-pollution of the soil by agrochemicals. It allows farmers to test samples of soil and then use global positioning systems (GPS) to direct their machines to the specific parts of fields that need fertilisers or pesticides. These state-of-the-art machines are very expensive and at present they are only used by the so-called 'barley barons' or agribusinesses. It is hoped, however, that smaller farms will either club together to buy and share the equipment or buy in the services of farm contractors.

*Paul Murphy/Fotolia*

**Figure 7.6**
*An end to ploughing?*

What all this means is that one of the classic features of the UK countryside — the ploughed field (Figure 7.6) — will become a rare sight. But this could be a small price to pay for managing our soil in a sustainable way.

# Concerns about the Gene Revolution

In Part 6 we noted concerns about GM crops and what their environmental impacts might be. The warnings of the Argentinian experience need to be heeded. It may be that GM crops are a non-starter in the race for sustainable sources of food.

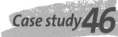 *Case study* **46** | WARNINGS FROM ARGENTINA

### Too sold on soya beans

Soya beans contain all three of the macronutrients required for good nutrition and are an important source of vegetable oil and protein. They are also used to make soy sauce, and the oil derived from them is used in many branches of manufacturing. However, in recent years, the incentive to grow soya beans has been boosted by the fact that they can yield a biofuel capable of being burnt in a diesel engine.

Argentina is the world's third-largest producer of soya beans, after the USA and Brazil. The area given over to the growth of GM soya has increased from 0.01 million to over

*Contemporary Case Studies*

14 million hectares in 30 years. The underlying reason has been the country's massive debts and the fact that the global price of soya has made it a very profitable export. But the improvement of the country's balance of payments has not been without its costs.

Argentina's production of soya has been largely based on the genetically engineered glyphosate herbicide-resistant Roundup Ready soya bean developed by Monsanto. But some worrying warnings are beginning to show:

- The growth of GM soya has meant an increasing use of glyphosate herbicides. This, in turn, has resulted in an accelerating development of herbicide-resistant weeds. Insects have emerged that do significant damage to the soya bean, so increasingly heavy applications of insecticides have been necessary. Furthermore, the emergence of soya bean rust now requires widespread use of fungicide. In short, all three applications are seriously threatening biodiversity.

- Argentina's agriculture has moved closer to being a monoculture. This inevitably makes the whole agricultural system very vulnerable. It would only need a downward shift in the global price or some natural catastrophe and Argentina would be in even deeper trouble.

- The rise in soya bean production has led to massive increases in hunger and malnutrition in a country that used to produce ten times as much food as the population consumed. The consequences of growing GM soya have included a massive exodus of people from the countryside. Land once used for growing basic food crops has been turned over to the cultivation of soya beans, thereby threatening national food security.

- Not so long ago, Argentina was one of the world's major livestock producers. The Argentinian people were renowned as great meat-eaters. Now, however, they are being pressured by the government to eat soya as an alternative to their traditional diet. It is a change that the Argentinians are finding difficult to swallow!

*The case of GM soya bean production in Argentina raises some concerns — environmental, economic and social. The most worrying aspect is the serious decline in the country's food security resulting from its obsession with GM soya. Argentina needs to diversify.*

## 39 Question

**Explain the concerns that people have about the growing of GM crops.**

### Guidance

Concerns include: food safety, 'genetic contamination', heavy use of herbicides, loss of biodiversity, displacement of subsistence/food crops by monoculture of one GM crop, and power of biotech TNCs.

*Using case studies*

# Food or biofuel?

Today's world is becoming increasingly concerned about three commodities — food, water and energy. There are some important interconnections here that have their tensions. Food crops need water, but water is also needed to generate energy.

Food production requires farmland, but the demand for energy is leading to an increasing use of land to produce biofuels.

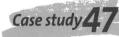 

## A QUESTION FOR THE WHOLE WORLD

### Food or biofuel?

Replacing fossil oil with biofuels such as ethanol and biodiesel has its appeal. Since these biofuels are derived from agricultural crops, they are readily renewable. Ethanol and biodiesel emit less particulate pollution than oil-based petroleum and diesel. Furthermore, biofuels do not contribute to global warming, since they only release into the atmosphere the carbon dioxide that their source plants absorbed from the atmosphere in the first place. But despite this, biofuels are not carbon neutral, because it requires energy to grow the crops and convert them into fuel. The amount of fuel used during this production (to power machinery, to transport crops etc.) does have a large impact on the overall savings achieved by biofuels (Figure 7.7). However, biofuels are substantially more environmentally friendly than some of their energy alternatives.

*Figure 7.7*
*Biofuels life cycle*

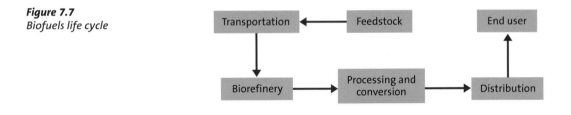

No one denies that biofuels have an increasingly important role to play in reducing carbon dioxide emissions. For example, they can reduce carbon emissions by up to 60% compared with fossil fuels. Not just that, but increasing use of biofuels will reduce our dependence on diminishing stocks of fossil fuels. An added attraction of biodiesel is that we can fill our existing car or domestic heating oil tank with it. No major changes need to be made to our cars, buses, lorries or domestic heating systems.

While everything about biofuels appears very rosy from an energy point of view, there is a huge fly in the ointment as far as the growth of biofuel crops is concerned. The principal sources to date are sugar cane, sugar beet, sorghum and maize for ethanol, and oilseed rape, jatropha, palm oil and soya bean for biodiesel. Four of these crops (sugar cane, sorghum, jatropha and palm oil) grow best in tropical latitudes, while the remaining four grow best in temperate latitudes. The problem really concerns those grown in the tropics. Growing these crops promises developing countries money-earning exports as well as employment. However, finding the land on which to grow these crops is the issue. That land can generally only be brought into cultivation in one of three ways:

- by the acquisition of subsistence farmland
- by the conversion of commercial farms from food to biofuels
- by deforestation (*Case study 31*)

The first is highly likely to enhance food insecurity (*Case study 3*), while the third promises irreparable damage to the environment.

The only really sustainable course of action here is to shift the onus of biofuel cultivation to the temperate or developed world. After all, that is the part of the world that will benefit most from biofuels. Why should the developing world grow these crops and become even hungrier?

*Few would challenge the argument that biofuels have an important and sustainable role to play in reducing reliance on fossil fuels. But the growth of biofuel crops threatens food supplies, particularly in areas that are already short of food.*

---

**Using case studies**

**40**

Compile a two-column table that identifies the costs and benefits a developing country in the tropics might experience as a result of growing biofuel crops.

**Guidance**

Work under four sub-headings: environmental, economic, social and political.

---

The hope is that the need for biofuels will become so acute and the price so high that the producer countries will be able to afford global food prices. But in terms of food security, it is a second-best option to that of self-sufficiency.

# Land grabbing and outsourcing

The next case study serves as a timely warning that the idea that developing countries can be made more food-secure by a wholesale switch from subsistence to commercial agriculture is fundamentally flawed. No one would deny developing countries the chance to progress in terms of economic development, but the switch to commercial food production is not the way to go. It is certainly not a sustainable pathway.

---

## A TRAIL OF STARVATION AND FOOD INSECURITY

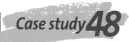
Case study **48**

### The consequences of land grabbing and outsourcing

The acquisition of farmland from some of the poorest people in the world by rich countries and TNCs is accelerating at an alarming rate. For example, it is estimated that at least 30 million hectares are being acquired to grow food for countries such as China and the Gulf states that cannot grow enough food for their populations. Land is also being acquired for outsourcing the growth of biofuels. In some cases, land is even being acquired for its water resources. The UN believes that this land grabbing will seriously reduce the ability of poor countries to feed themselves. Critics call the practice a blatant form of neo-colonialism.

---

*Food & Famine*

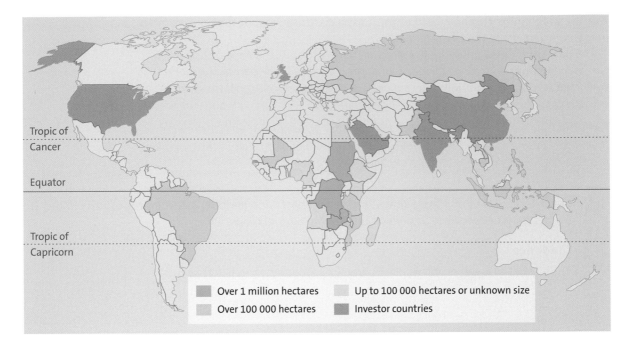

Over 1 million hectares     Up to 100 000 hectares or unknown size

Over 100 000 hectares     Investor countries

**Figure 7.8**
*Buying foreign fields in 2009*

Figure 7.8 provides a global picture of this land grabbing. The countries that are being targeted include not only fertile countries such as Brazil, Russia and the Ukraine, but also poor countries such as Cameroon, Ethiopia, Madagascar and Zambia.

One analyst has summed up the consequences of this land grabbing and outsourcing as follows:

> Outsourcing food production will ensure food security for investing countries, but would leave behind a trail of hunger, starvation and food scarcities for local populations. The environmental tab of highly intensive farming — devastated soils, dry aquifers and ruined ecology from chemical infestation — will be left for the host country to pick up.

Increased investment by the outsourcing countries may bring benefits to the host countries such as GDP growth and greater government revenues, as well as economic development and improvements in the quality of life of some. But this investment will also result in local people losing access to the resources on which they depend for their food security.

*Land grabbing and outsourcing are evidence of the inequality of our world. Included in the costs that host countries will have to pick up is increased food insecurity.*

**41**

**Using case studies**

**Make a case in support of land grabbing and outsourcing.**

### Guidance

Initially, view the activities through the eyes of the commissioning country. Then identify possible advantages for a host country. It will give your response more bite if you focus on two specific countries (one commissioner and one host).

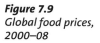

We conclude this part of the book with a reminder, should we need it, that all is not well in our world. In 2008 there were food riots in Egypt, Mexico, Haiti and even the USA as the prices of basic foodstuffs surged to record levels. Although it started in the banking world, the credit crunch had a significant impact on global agricultural markets and food prices during 2007–08 (Figure 7.9). The global financial crisis has revealed the high risks associated with the promotion of commercial food production in the developing world. It was advocated on the basis that it promised to deliver regular employment and wages, but the reality is that this is only the case when the global economy is booming. Abandoning subsistence farming in favour of commercial crop production and becoming involved as a host to outsourcing increase reliance on food produced by other people and most likely in other countries. In short, poor people are held to ransom when global food prices rise. The degrees of food insecurity and food entitlement deficits are inevitably raised.

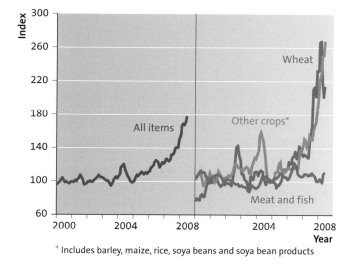

*Includes barley, maize, rice, soya beans and soya bean products

**Figure 7.9**
*Global food prices, 2000–08*

### 42 Question

Which of the commodity price rises in Figure 7.9 do you think had the greatest impact on food insecurity?

### Guidance

You will need to consider which of these foods is the staple for the greatest number of people.

*Using case studies*

The fact that we in the UK have been able to ponder tomorrow's food security (*Case study 42*) is something of a luxury compared with the plight of millions of people in many countries who are unable to look beyond surviving today. It is indeed an unequal and unjust world when enough food is produced for everyone (there is no overall food availability deficit), yet a significant proportion of the population faces hunger and famine (there are glaring food entitlement deficits). It may well be that over the next 50 years the world will raise its overall production of food to still higher levels, and perhaps do so in a more sustainable way. But will the levels of hunger and famine show commensurate decreases? The rate of future population growth will be critical. So too will be the nature of economic globalisation — it needs to become much more humanitarian and much more focused on reducing inequalities.

# Examination advice

The case studies that form an integral part of your A-level geography course are included principally to illustrate and help you understand theoretical ideas and particular contemporary issues. The same case studies also serve a third purpose, namely to be put to good use in a variety of ways in the examination. Much depends on the question task and the command used in the wording of a question. Table 8.1 indicates that there are at least four different question scenarios. They are ranked according to what is expected in terms of the degree of case study detail. They range from simple name-dropping to a detailed knowledge and understanding of a particular situation, issue or idea.

Much depends also on the context of the question — the challenge is to find an example or case study that is appropriate to the question topic. Table 8.2 may help here, for it links the 48 case studies presented in this book to the main topic areas of the human food chain.

*Table 8.1*
*Question commands and the examiner's case study and text expectations*

**Increasing requirement for case study detail**

| Task or command* | Name | Support | Compare | Examine (a particular situation or statement) |
|---|---|---|---|---|
| **Typical question** | Give an example of a country with a high level of food insecurity | With the use of examples, show how food production threatens the natural environment | Evaluate the causes of food insecurity in two named countries | With reference to a named country or region, examine the main factors affecting its level of food security |
| **Case study expectation** | No more than the name of an appropriate country — e.g. Ethiopia | Use of at least two contrasting case studies — might be countries or, perhaps better, processes (salinisation and deforestation) | Try to opt for two contrasting case studies — e.g. Ethiopia (largely natural causes) and Zimbabwe (largely human causes) | A simple diagram showing the salient factors would be helpful; a systematic look at key factors should follow |
| **Text requirement** | One sentence | Two or three sentences per example | Extended prose | In-depth extended prose |

* A word of caution — watch out for those questions that do not specifically ask for examples, but nonetheless expect them. For example:
- Suggest reasons why some natural hazards lead to famine.
- 'GM crops create as many problems as they solve.' Discuss.
- To what extent do you agree with the view that the global food problem results from the mismatch between food production and food consumption?

If you are in doubt as to whether examples are required in your answer to a question, it is better give some rather than none, but not of the 'e.g. Africa' kind!

**Table 8.2** *Case studies and figures in this book and the main topics of the human food chain to which they relate*

| Topic | See Case study/ Figure | Topic | See Case study/ Figure |
|---|---|---|---|
| **Food production** | | **Food security and insecurity** | |
| 1 Technological advances | 1, 36 | 1 The global pattern of food security | 9, 10 |
| 2 The global pattern of food supply | 4, 5 | 2 The global pattern of hunger | 11 |
| 3 Food production systems | 2, 3, 4, 5 | 3 Population and resources | 12 |
| 4 Environmental impacts | 30, 31, 32, 33, 34, 35 | 4 Causes of food insecurity | 11, 12, 13, 14, 15 |
| 5 Changes in food supply | 1, 3, 6, 41, 47 | 5 Famine | 16, 17, 18, 19, 21, 22, 23 |
| 6 Sustainable ways of raising production | 38, 39, 40, 45 | 6 Aid | 20, 41 |
| **Food consumption** | | **Power players in the human food chain** | |
| 1 Development and rising living standards | 6 | 1 Governments | 4, 6, 17, 18, 19, 24, 26 |
| 2 Undernutrition | 7, 11, 12, 13, 14 | 2 Agribusinesses | 25 |
| 3 Overnutrition | 8 | 3 Global trade | 26, 41, 48 |
| 4 Food miles | 34, 48 | 4 TNCs | 29 |
| 5 Diet and health issues | 6, 8, 21, 43, 44 | 5 Supermarkets and fast-food chains | 27, 28 |
| 6 Controlling consumption | 42, 48 | 6 Future challenges | 36, 46, 47, 48 |

We will now look at five different examination contexts that require the use of case studies. Four are shown in Table 8.1: they apply mainly to unseen examination papers. The fifth is where the geography specification requires you to undertake an enquiry into a set topic and to submit a report by a given deadline. So those contexts range from simply naming a case study as an example of a particular situation, through use of case study material for support purposes, to an extended and detailed use of case studies.

# Naming examples

This requires nothing more than being able to cite one of your case studies as a relevant example. The test here is basically one of appropriateness. In part (b) of the sample question below, it would suffice to simply name any food-insecure country, such as Ethiopia or Haiti.

**43** | **Question**

(a) **Identify three symptoms of food insecurity.**
(b) **Name one country that is widely recognised as being food-insecure. Give reasons for your choice.**

**Guidance**

(a) Malnutrition/starvation, widespread poverty, high incidence of disease.
(b) China, Ethiopia, Indonesia, Puerto Rico, Haiti. Reasons — high scoring in terms of indicator measures.

*Using case studies*

# Naming and using a supporting example

The next level up requires that you do more than just name an appropriate example. You will also be expected to demonstrate knowledge and understanding by providing a little detail.

**44**

**Using case studies**

### Question

**With reference to a named 'dryland' country,**
**(a) suggest possible indicators of the degree of food insecurity**
**(b) outline the factors that contribute to the food insecurity**
**(c) suggest one sustainable development action that might help reduce the level of food insecurity**

### Guidance

Any one of the Sahel countries will suffice — Ethiopia, Sudan, Niger etc.

(a) daily calorie intake, infant mortality rate, aid receipts

(b) overpopulation, civil war, poor government, desertification, climate change

(c) water conservation (need to maximise sustainable use of this scarce resource), permaculture, reduction in numbers of livestock

# Using case studies comparatively

Essay-type questions that require the comparative use of case studies are popular with chief examiners. Much of the challenge of such questions hinges on selecting appropriate case studies. In some instances, the choice is fairly obvious and restricted. In others, there may be more options than you might think from an initial reading of the question. Look at 'Using case studies 45'.

**45**

**Using case studies**

### Question

**With reference to two contrasting** (key word) **examples, evaluate** (command word) **the impact of government intervention** (key words) **on food production** (key words).

### Guidance

It is always worth 'editing' the question by highlighting key words and command words.

The obvious choice here is to compare government intervention in a capitalist country with that in a socialist country. One of the countries involved in the EU CAP (*Case study 24*) or the USA (*Case study 4*) would be two immediate candidates as representatives of the capitalist 'camp'. For the socialist 'camp', Russia (*Case study 5*), China (*Case studies 5 and 6*) or North Korea (*Case study 19*) would suffice.

Hold on a moment and take another and closer look at the question. There is nothing here to say that your answer can only be about two contrasting politico-economic regimes. It would be quite legitimate to take one country where there has been virtually no government intervention at all (say Ethiopia or Niger). Another criterion for selecting the two countries could be the precise objectives of the intervention: raising food production, reducing it, protecting domestic agriculture against foreign imports etc. In this case, it would be appropriate to choose two countries that had different intervention intentions, say the UK (curtailing) and India (increasing).

Having made the important decision about exemplar countries, we now come to the critical part of the question — the evaluation. Any evaluation requires first that you clearly establish what the objectives of the intervention were. Each country would need to be evaluated separately. This should be followed by a conclusion indicating which country you think has been more successful in achieving its aims.

The trouble with all examination questions that ask you to compare situations (as represented by appropriate case studies) is that most candidates believe that all they have to do is to rehash each in turn. What this really means is that examiners are left to draw their own conclusions as to whether or not the situations are similar. In short, the question is not answered and relatively few marks will be gained. In planning effective answers to the comparative type of question, it is necessary to interleave rather than block references to your chosen case studies.

# Building an essay around a single case study

A successful attempt to answer any question that starts, 'With reference to a named country…' will require you to:
- choose an appropriate country
- have a sufficiently detailed knowledge of that country relevant to the thrust of the particular question
- resist the temptation to set down literally all that you know about your chosen country (the 'kitchen sink' approach), but instead harness only those aspects that are directly relevant

## Question

**For a named country, identify the consequences of overnutrition.**

## Guidance

The UK (*Case study 8*) should help you tackle this question. Here is a checklist of possible consequences. The generic headings should give your answer both structure and coherence:

**Physiological and medical**
- high incidence of overweight and obese people
- high risk of a range of illnesses and early death

The consequences below are essentially the repercussions of the previous bullet point.

**Economic**

- productivity of labour force reduced by days off for ill-health
- labour force deprived of the experience of older workers who die before reaching the age of retirement
- capacity of public transport reduced by having to accommodate larger and therefore fewer people
- coping with obesity — larger clothing sizes, stronger beds and chairs

**Social**

- overstretched health service
- premature deaths lead to break-up of families and higher incidence of orphans

# Planning an extended essay or report involving a range of case studies

The standard advice on essay planning should be followed, namely that the essay should have a three-part structure — a brief introduction and an equally brief conclusion (say one paragraph each) separated by a series of paragraphs (the expansion) that develop your argument or discussion points. It is here that you will need to incorporate supporting examples and case studies.

**47**

*Using case studies*

## Question

**Which do you think poses the greater challenge to a developing country** (define) **— the commercialisation of agriculture** (define) **or the introduction of GM crops** (define)**? Justify your viewpoint with reference to examples.**

## Guidance

### Introduction

Rather than jumping in at the deep end and naming your choice, perhaps you should be a little more subtle.

Certainly start by defining terms (as indicated). Perhaps follow this by making the point that both developments are likely to be introduced as ways of increasing food production, but not necessarily for the benefit of the country's people. It will also pay off if you attempt to justify your choice of case studies to follow.

### Expansion

Look at the likely aims of each development and their particular challenges.

Commercialisation of agriculture (use *Case studies 3, 15 and 48*):

- Aims: to provide foreign capital through the export of crops; employment; regular wages; a basis for economic development etc.

- Challenges: how to feed people who transfer from subsistence farming and sell their land; how to protect these people from food prices rising above wage levels; how to guarantee access to markets in the developed world; how to overcome seasonality of demand etc.

GM crops (use *Case studies 36 and 46*):
- Aims: could be to help make subsistence farmers more food-secure or to boost production of crops for export.
- Challenges: success with GM crops requires access to relatively high technology; might be available to commercial farmers but unlikely in the case of subsistence farmers. In the former case, it is tempting to overspecialise in crops that currently command high prices. Still many 'unknowns' as to the possible impacts of GM crops.

### Conclusion

Provided you have made your evaluations as you have considered each development, you can save your weighing-up of the two challenges for the conclusion. You might conclude that turning to commercial agriculture presents the greater challenge because once people are not producing their own food, they become vulnerable to hikes in global food prices. If the technological and cost requirements can be reduced, GM crops could undoubtedly help raise subsistence food production.

# Detecting bias in case studies

Just as we live in an unfair world, we should always be alive to the fact that what we are reading is not always fair. Writers often write from a personal viewpoint, and as a result what they produce is almost invariably biased towards that viewpoint. Rarely is a particular issue viewed evenly from a range of different viewpoints. It is particularly important when reading case study material to be constantly alive to possible bias — first identify it and then decide what needs to be said to give it balance and a sense of evenness and fairness.

48

**Select a case study in this book that you think shows bias. Identify the bias and then suggest what needs to be done to make it fairer.**

### Guidance

Since this task is likely to expose me as a compiler of biased case studies, you will receive no help from me! Get on and do it yourself.

Grasping and applying the advice contained in this final part of the book should have a positive outcome. It is sometimes easy to forget that the subject of geography is the real world. The more contemporary examples you can include in your examination work, the more you are likely to convince and impress the examiner that you have a sound knowledge and understanding of today's world. In short, a good dose of reality in the form of relevant case studies and examples can work wonders when it comes to improving your AS and A2 geography grades.

*Using case studies*

# Index

*Contemporary Case Studies*